GOD'S LAVISH GRACE

By the same author:

God's Lavish Grace

"A refreshing contrast to the man-centred gospel . . .
Few books come along that I could recommend
so wholeheartedly."
– Revd. Dr R T Kendall

TERRY VIRGO

MONARCH
BOOKS

Oxford, UK, and Grand Rapids, Michigan

First published in the UK 2004 by Monarch Books
(a publishing imprint of Lion Hudson plc),
Wilkinson House, Jordan Hill House, Oxford, OX2 8DR.
Tel: +44 (0) 1865 302750 Fax: +44 (0) 1865 302757
Email: monarch@lionhudson.com
www.lionhudson.com

Reprinted 2005, 2007, 2010, 2011

ISBN: 978 1 85424 645 5 (UK)
ISBN: 978 0 8254 6053 1 (USA)

Distributed by:
UK: Marston Book Services, PO Box 269,
Abingdon, Oxon OX14 4YN;
USA: Kregel Publications, PO Box 2607
Grand Rapids, Michigan 49501.

Unless otherwise stated, Scripture quotations are
taken from the Holy Bible, New American Standard Bible,
© The Lockman Foundation 1960, 1962, 1963, 1968, 1971,
1972, 1973, 1975, 1977. All rights reserved.

NIV = New International Version
© 1973, 1978, 1984 by the International Bible Society.

This book has been printed on paper and board independently
certified as having come from sustainable forests.

British Library Cataloguing Data
A catalogue record for this book is available
from the British Library.

Printed and bound in Great Britain by Clays Ltd, St Ives plc.

Contents

Contents

Acknowledgements

I owe a huge debt of gratitude to those who have helped shape and confirm my thinking on the theme of grace, through their writing, speaking and liberated lives. I thank God for each one of them.

I am also profoundly grateful to God for the privilege of being rooted in a grace-filled church. The Church of Christ the King in Brighton has been my home for 25 years now and from there I have had the privilege of travelling widely to share this message. *Newfrontiers* is a family of churches that I have now been serving for over 30 years. They are scattered among the nations and celebrating the grace of God, expressing worship, works and witness that testify to the goodness of that grace; I am deeply grateful to everyone in that ever-expanding family.

Finally, I want to express genuine, heartfelt gratitude to Janis Peters, my secretary, who has typed and retyped the manuscript of this book. Her efficiency and wonderful enthusiasm have made it possible to bring this material to you in its present form.

Preface

I had been a Christian for about 16 years before my eyes were opened to the truth of God's grace in a life-changing way.

My experience as a Christian began with five years of backsliding followed by about eleven years of zealous but rather condemnation-driven Christianity. I became increasingly involved in serving God and left my secular work to take up full-time evangelism, followed by Bible College and then some years of pastoral ministry.

One day, I seemed to see some bright sky among the clouds above me, but it quickly closed. I momentarily thought that I heard God tell me that I did not have to earn his love but that he loved me freely and always would! But it was too good to be true and I returned to my former attitude based on duty, applied zeal, passion for God and fervour to serve him, mixed with frequent condemnation.

Some time later, the clouds opened again and I was sure that I had seen something new and gloriously releasing! I began to grasp the wonder of his glorious grace. I gave myself to fresh study and then began to preach God's grace with new freedom, joy and certainty, having personally experienced the complete transformation of my own Christian life.

It has now been my joy and privilege for a number of years to proclaim the grace of God in many nations, and it has also been my delight to see many lives transformed through this wonderful life-changing truth. Few joys can be compared with discovering the wonder of God's grace, and I now set this material before you, certain that, if you will give yourself to reading it with an open heart and a willing spirit, your whole experience of Christ can also be transformed. You can be set free to enjoy his grace, to celebrate his love, to be certain of your freely-given righteousness, and to make him known to others.

God's grace defies our comprehension. His kindness is unfathomable, his covenant love unbreakable. May you encounter the love of God in a new and releasing way as you read the volume in your hands.

Terry Virgo
January 2004

1

The way in

Maybe you are one of the many Christians who wish that you were more fulfilled in your walk with God. Perhaps you wonder if you are doing enough to deserve his pleasure and earn his acceptance: clouds of condemnation trouble you even when you try to pray. Reading the Bible may have become a chore rather than a pleasure.

How do you get out of this vicious circle of trying harder, followed by disappointment and despondency? Is there something you have failed to understand, a key that can open a new door for you?

This opening chapter shows the way out of the bondage of law-keeping into a fruitful life where you enjoy the grace of God.

The way in

It really does depend on whom you know. I was standing
with Wendy, my wife, in Washington DC on Pennsylvania
Avenue looking up at the White House. I had reason to
hope that I might actually enter the place and have a look
around its inner recesses. We had arrived with a promise but
with considerable uncertainty as to how things would work.
As Wendy and I drew close to the railings around the gar-
den area of the magnificent building, we were approached
by a very large policeman and, unlike English policemen, he
was well armed with a sizeable gun on his hip. He enquired
where we thought we might be going. I rather tentatively
replied that we had hoped to enter the White House.

He looked at me rather pityingly and made it very clear to
this foolish Englishman that no one walked into the White
House.

I explained to him that I was a preacher and that in the
morning I had preached at the Covenant Life Church in
nearby Gaithersburg and had been assured that I would be
able to gain access to the White House through a man who
was a member of that church.

"And who is this guy?" he enquired.

"I think his name is John," I replied pathetically.

Perhaps I had never felt so disqualified from the hope of realising any previous ambition I might have had. At this very moment John arrived. Hurriedly jumping from a cab, he ran to our side. Actually, I did not know his face since I had never met him. He was simply a member of the large congregation where I had preached in the morning but he had been given clear instruction and had arrived to meet Wendy and me and take us into the White House. He presented his credentials to the officer who checked them on his computer in a nearby cabin and, wonder of wonders, the gate opened and we walked in, not only to the grounds but also to the inner recesses of the White House. We were told that there were two possible tours, one of which was the VIP one, surpassing the normal public one. But we were privileged to go beyond even the VIP tour and were taken into the Cabinet Office and even to the doorway of the Oval Office. A very kind guard explained to us many of the details of things placed around the office and even those which were on President Reagan's desk. It was a high privilege.

It was wonderful to gain access through the person in whom we put our trust.

Paul tells us that being justified by faith we have peace with God through our Lord Jesus Christ, through whom we have also obtained our introduction by faith into this grace in which we stand (see Romans 5:1–2). God has provided one who can give us access to grace.

We shall always remember our visit to the White House, but of course it was only a visit. Jesus brought us into a place where we can stand permanently. We stand in grace through the access that he has gained for us. Jesus not only rescues us from the wrath to come, he not only forgives us our sins, but he has obtained for us a place to stand in grace, a place of total acceptance and security, fully qualified and not fearing sudden disqualification or forced removal. His credentials overcome all the barriers that stood against us.

No need to search the depths of our hearts for arguments to force our entry. The only way in is through his perfect righteousness, and having gained entry we must learn to *stand* in grace.

Reigning in life

In the same chapter (Romans 5:17) Paul speaks of the great prospect of our "reigning in life". Similar promises are that Christ will always lead us in triumph (2 Corinthians 2:14) and that we overwhelmingly conquer through him who loved us (Romans 8:37). These exciting phrases describe the normal Christian life. However, they often leave us feeling condemned rather than encouraged, knowing that we fall terribly short of what is promised. Often we are brought face to face with the fact that we are hardly "reigning in life". Too often we feel we are losers rather than winners, overruled rather than reigning, at the mercy of depression and dejection and the sense of unworthiness before God; in fact, let's face it, condemned!

"If only I could reign in life" is what we feel. Sometimes we are brought to a spiritual crisis in our lives, maybe at a special event when we are exposed to a very searching sermon. Once again we repent, asking God for mercy and, if our response is wholehearted, we may even follow through with fresh determination. Sometimes we face this at the beginning of a new year, when, after a year of being in the spiritual doldrums, we embrace the challenge of a fresh January 1st. Maybe someone has given us a new diary for Christmas. Every page is virgin white and unspoiled. We haven't yet wrecked this new year or any day of it. If only I could do better. If only I could reign in life. If only I could be a conqueror. Why can't I be a winner and not a loser?

Sadly, at this very moment, many a Christian takes a step which is rooted in genuine aspiration to do better but actually is a sad step through a wrong door, along a wrong path. Forgetting to read what the text actually says about "reigning in life", we tend to set ourselves targets to live by, as though that was the secret. We might choose to set our alarm clock one hour earlier in the morning and determine that we will pray more fervently and in a more disciplined way. We might then think that this year I will read my Bible right through from cover to cover. I will start a new reading plan. Furthermore, I shall witness to one person each day. I make it my resolve. I must do better. If I can only obey these rules that I set myself, I can learn to reign in life. If only I could live by these laws life would be so different.

You may even enjoy a few good days but before January has reached double figures, the very laws you have set yourself are turning on you to condemn you that you are already a few days behind in your Bible reading and that you have slept through your prayer time, or even knelt but found no motivation, no sense of fellowship with God and only a dreadful feeling of anguish that you don't really know how to pray. Your spiritual endeavours seem to make you feel even more disqualified, since they bring you no joy. Where on earth have you gone wrong? Why is it so difficult to live the Christian life?

One of your problems is that you did not look closely at the text that promises that you will "reign in life" (Romans 5:17). It does not actually speak about your spiritual work rate or your personal endeavour. It certainly does not speak about imposing laws upon yourself to help you pick yourself up by your own shoelaces. Rather the opposite! It tells you that through receiving the abundance of grace and the free gift of righteousness, you reign in life through the one Christ Jesus.

Your position not your performance

You reign in life by receiving abundant grace, not by putting yourself under laws. It is because of your standing that you reign in life. It is because you have obtained grace, not because you have achieved or accomplished merit. It is by your position, not by your performance! The imposition of law upon your life will never cause you to reign in life. It will never cause you to enjoy fellowship with Jesus and the grace-filled life that is so necessary for you to bear fruit for God.

From the outset it is crucial for you to understand your place in relationship to law. The apostle Paul wants you to be quite certain of this. "You are not under law but under grace" (Romans 6:14). He tells us that "Christ is the end of the law so that there may be righteousness for everyone who believes" (Romans 10:4). In his most extended treatment of the subject of law (namely Romans 7), Paul sets out in vivid imagery your former relationship to law and the fact that God in his kind mercy has delivered you absolutely from its oppressive reign.

In the opening verses of Romans 7, Paul describes his readers as being married to the law. The law is pictured as an overbearing husband from whom there seems to be no escape. Since you are already married to the law, you are certainly not free to choose another husband, for that would be adultery. You cannot simply choose to become part of the bride of Christ and claim Jesus as your husband. You already have a husband, namely the law, who has absolute authority over you as long as you live. His repeated clear commands make his requirements very clear and leave you very conscious of your constant failure.

Sadly, this husband seems to communicate little kindness. He simply shows you your error and your serious shortcomings. He forever points out your impurities and inadequacies. He is an unattractive husband since, although his standards are high and his insistence that you keep those standards is constantly brought to your attention, he never lifts a finger to help you. This husband never comes to your aid. He never says, "Let me give you a hand." He merely stands rock-like, carved in stone, telling you what you should and shouldn't do. No point in arguing with him, because in your heart you know he is absolutely right. His standards are pure and holy. You cannot find fault in them. They are even strangely attractive, but oh so far out of sight in terms of daily fulfilment.

So now you are joined to a husband who makes you feel wretched and disqualified. While he lives, you can never marry another and, as if to destroy all possible hope of a joyful future, Jesus tells you that the law will never pass away. The law will never die. This husband is going to live forever! The door of hope is slammed in your face. You are permanently married to an overbearing, fault-finding husband who will never lift a finger to help you and he is never going to die. What a prospect! What terrible captivity! What wretchedness to live with!

Suddenly, Paul turns the argument "on its head" by telling us *not* that the law will pass away but that through the death of Christ – or more particularly "through His body" – you have "died to the law"! (Romans 7:4) He will never die but, through your identification with Christ, through your calling upon him to save you, through your appeal to a Christ who suffered on the cross and through believing in his shed blood, you are freely justified and included mysteriously in Christ where, from God's perspective, you are said to have died with him. Paul, therefore, makes a categorical statement that you have once and for all died to the law. Your former husband has not died but you have! You are released from him and his control.

In Romans 7:6 Paul continues the theme by telling you that you are indeed discharged from his authority, rather like someone who has been conscripted into national military service for a season, but now, having fulfilled his time, is then discharged from the army. He walks out free, no longer under its control. One can imagine a sergeant major seeing a discharged soldier and not realising that he has been discharged. The free man is strolling across the parade ground without a tie, and with a jacket slung over his shoulder, whistling as he walks in glorious freedom and abandon. The sergeant major, seeing this slovenly soldier, screams at him, expecting to impose his authority once more and call him to order. Imagine the glorious liberty of the discharged soldier merely saying, "Goodbye, Sarge!" Imagine every vein in the neck of the sergeant major standing out as he screams his commands on the deaf ears of the discharged soldier over whom he now has no authority whatever. The soldier is discharged. You are also discharged from the law, no longer under its control, no longer married to this particular husband.

But where does this leave you? Are you merely free-ranging? Can you now stroll around as you please, free from rules, regulations and laws to live by? Paul does not leave you in such a condition. He goes on to explain that having died to the law through the body of Christ, you are "joined to another, to Him who was raised from the dead in order that we might bear fruit for God" (Romans 7:4). You are set free so that you might not simply live the "single life" but be married to "Him who was raised from the dead". There is no doubt who this one is. The Lord Jesus now presents himself as a bridegroom, powerfully alive from the dead! Having been freed from slavery to the law, you can run into the arms of a totally new kind of husband, one full of grace and kindness.

Freed from an impotent husband

Not only does Jesus receive you into his loving arms, he also introduces new possibilities for your life, namely that you might "bear fruit for God". Bearing fruit was not on offer in fellowship with your former husband. Fruitfulness was not a prospect. He merely gave you instructions, not life. He set standards rather than imparting ability. Indeed, in Galatians 3:21 Paul makes it very clear that "if a law had been given that was able to impart life, then righteousness would indeed have been based on law". Sadly, the law could not impart life! The law could describe the righteousness required but could not impart the life that would make it possible. The law was an impotent husband! He imparted no life and left you thoroughly frustrated.

If only law could impart life. If only the law could say, "You shall not bear false witness. You shall not steal. You shall not commit adultery", and by simply commanding us could thereby change us, there would certainly be no more need. Simply tell us the rules and we are changed. Simply give us the commands and we are transformed. But the law imparted no life. By telling us not to covet, the law did not stop our coveting.

In stark contrast, Jesus is offered to you as a life-imparting husband. If you are joined to him you can bear fruit for God. Jesus said, "Abide in me and I in you. As the branch cannot bear fruit of itself unless it abides in the vine, so neither can you unless you abide in me. I am the vine, you are the branches. He who abides in me and I in him, he bears much fruit" (John 15:4, 5). Jesus is a life-imparting husband. He welcomes you into a relationship of love that will cause you to bear fruit from within, changing you from the inside. His words are spirit and life. Reigning in life and standing in grace become real possibilities if you do not have to return to law. Paul assures you that sin shall not have dominion over you since you are not under law but under grace (Romans 6:14). So why did God give the law in the first place? What does the law accomplish?

Many would argue that of course the law cannot save you, but you must return to the law for your sanctification. Only grace can save, but law is required to shape you up and make you holy. The reality, of course, is totally the opposite. The law does not impart life; it does not produce righteousness. It cannot sanctify. Grace not only saves you, it will enable you to live the holy life. Indeed, until you are totally released from your bondage to law, you will never produce a holy life. As Paul argues in Galatians 5:1, "It was for freedom that Christ set us free; therefore keep standing firm and do not be subject again to a yoke of slavery." This verse, in its context, is clearly talking about slavery to law, not slavery to sin.

That being the case, we might ask why God gave us the law in the first place? If the law cannot produce holiness, what does the law accomplish? We shall address this theme in the next chapter.

2

So what is the law for?

If, as we have seen, the law cannot save you or sanctify you, why did God give it to us? The apostle Paul shows that the law is far from irrelevant and that it played a vital role of preparation. It overshadowed adolescent Israel, reveals our utter sinfulness and leads us to Christ.

So what is the law for?

Clearly, the law is not to be ignored and indeed will not pass away. Although the believer is no longer bound to the law, it is of crucial importance that you understand the law's role, particularly in the life of the unbeliever. As Paul said to Timothy, "We know that the law is good, if one uses it lawfully, realising the fact that law is not made for a righteous person but for those who are lawless and rebellious . . ." (1 Timothy 1:8, 9).

So what does the law accomplish? First, it brings clear demarcation regarding what is sin and what is not. The law draws the lines for us. Paul indicates, "through the law comes the knowledge of sin" (Romans 3:20), adding, "I would not have come to know sin except through the law" (Romans 7:7). Sin is not simply a social disorder but an offence against God. It is not a matter of common consent or a standard arrived at through social consensus. God defined the law and the law reveals sin.

Although we are gifted by God with a human conscience (a subject to which we will return later), the conscience is by no means infallible and can be abused and defiled. Conscience can be shaped by the changing fads of human society in terms of what becomes currently acceptable or unacceptable in the culture. We need something far more objective than conscience. We need a plumbline coming down out of heaven telling us the unchanging holy standard required. The law perfectly fulfils this role, making plain what is acceptable or unacceptable to God. The law, therefore, fulfils a crucial task of identifying sin.

Paul then goes on to make a rather unexpected statement, namely that the law also provokes sin. "Sin, taking opportunity through the commandment, produced in me coveting of every kind; for apart from the law sin is dead. I was once alive apart from the law; but when the commandment came, sin became alive, and I died; and this commandment, which was to result in life, proved to result in death for me; for sin, taking opportunity through the commandment, deceived me, and through it killed me" (Romans 7:8–11).

The law provokes sin

Amazingly, God's laws actually provoke human reaction rather than submissive obedience. Something in the human heart rebels against God's holy law. The commandment, which was supposed to produce life, actually produces rebellion and death. Fallen humanity hates to be told what to do. Newspapers often tell us that popular polls reveal that many still believe in God. The pollsters express surprise that things are plainly not as bad as people thought – the vast majority are still believers! People seem to be happy to tick the box indicating that they still have faith. God is not doing so badly in the popularity stakes after all – but what kind of God? Would their reply differ if another question were asked or indeed if they were confronted with the requirements of God, namely his holy law?

Few men and women will thank you for telling them that God says that they should have no other gods before him, that they should never lie, steal, commit adultery or covet other people's possessions. When the law's requirements are presented, "sin springs to life" (Romans 7:9). This can be demonstrated in the most trivial of ways. Even a command to "keep off the grass" can provoke resentment and rebellion. You may have had no intention of walking on the grass but suddenly you find yourself asking, "Why shouldn't I walk on the grass? Whose grass is it anyway?" The forbidden becomes strangely attractive and man's essential commitment to disobedience surfaces. The law, Paul argues, not only defines sin, it also provokes it.

Having shown us the law's potential for provoking evil, Paul is quick to uphold the law by telling us that "the law is holy, and the commandment is holy, righteous and good" (Romans 7:12). Paul does not want us to misunderstand, or think that he is himself anti-law. He knows "that the law is spiritual" (Romans 7:14) and "good" (Romans 7:16). But Paul goes on to demonstrate that God's purpose is to make it abundantly clear that man is truly in dire straits and in such a fallen condition that he needs more help than mere laws can provide. Indeed, man is so bad that he is not ultimately helped by receiving law.

Adding God's holy law makes us worse!

Paul takes his argument a step further in Romans 7:13 by asking, "Did that which is good become a cause of death to me? May it never be! Rather it was sin, in order that it might be shown to be sin by affecting my death through that which is good, so that through the commandment sin would become utterly sinful." This is a difficult verse, but one we must try to understand. God wants to make it abundantly clear that man in his sin is utterly sinful. Adding the law to him does not improve him but strangely makes him even worse.

Let me illustrate. Imagine someone being offered a glass of water to drink that is supposedly pure but not definitely so. Our expectation is that the glass contains good drinking water, but this has yet to be proven. Maybe we taste the water and think that it is probably good, but still we are unsure. It is then suggested that we add something to the water which we know is pure and good, unquestionably unadulterated. We would expect that in adding what is certainly good we would improve the quality of the water and so we add the pure and good, anticipating a good result.

We then taste the new mixture and to our utter amazement the drink is now revolting and disgusting. Huge questions now arise. How could something that seemed to be OK, which now has been added to by something that is undoubtedly pure and good, now be discovered to be totally undrinkable? What have we learned from our experiment? Because we know that what we added was undoubtedly good, we have learned that the original drink must have been a lot worse than we had ever imagined. Though the water was masquerading as already good, the addition of the undoubtedly good uncovered the reality. This is bad water!

Paul's argument is that God's intention was that sin should be seen to be utterly sinful. God wanted to make it very clear that man is not essentially good and simply needing better education or nobler rules. He has demonstrated that if you add to natural man a law that is holy, pure and good, the result is not improvement but rebellion, enmity and death. The law does not come to save us but to show us our need of a Saviour. Satan wants to trick us into trying to prove ourselves holy by the law which God gave to prove us sinners. The law came to rub it in. Jesus came to rub it out.

To lead us to Christ

Paul argues in Galatians, "the law was put in charge to lead us to Christ" (Galatians 3:24, NIV). He wrote them his most animated letter, addressing them, according to J B Phillips, as "you dear idiots!" (Galatians 3:1) (J B Phillips, *Letters to*

Young Churches, Fontana, 1947). Paul had enjoyed a very successful evangelistic outreach into Galatia, seeing many saved and forming a church that was flooded with the Spirit and experiencing miraculous signs (see Galatians 3:5).

Having established a vibrant New Testament community, Paul moved on, only to receive news that this young church had received into their midst Judaising teachers who wanted to impose law on these new converts. The Jews understood that one day the far off nations would see the light; the Gentiles would ultimately abandon their idols and come to embrace the Jewish God, as their prophets had promised. Some Jewish Christians reckoned that they knew what was required of these new converts. They realised that for centuries God's requirement had been the keeping of the law, the observing of the Sabbath, the need for circumcision, the embracing of food laws.

Now these new Gentile converts who had embraced the God of Israel needed to be taught how to add the law to their new-found faith. In Paul's absence the Galatians had succumbed to this distortion of the gospel and were beginning to embrace these outward religious signs, which Paul regarded as mere works of the flesh and as "falling from grace" (Galatians 5:4). It was very clear to Paul that the law had done its job by pointing out man's sinful need and directing us to Christ. There was certainly no need now to return to the law once its job was complete. To do so was to undermine the gospel and, indeed, to preach what Paul unashamedly called another gospel, which was no gospel at all! (Galatians 1:6–7)

Full rights as sons

Paul's perspective was that, while the people of Israel were adolescent and indeed mere children, they needed to be overseen by the law. As he says in Galatians 3:23, "Before faith came, we were kept in custody under the law, being shut up to the faith which was later to be revealed." The law was a temporary measure, keeping guard over the infant people of God.

However, when the fullness of time came, God sent forth his son, born of a woman, born under the law, so that he might redeem those who were under the law that we might receive the adoption of sons (Galatians 4:4, 5). In the ancient world, adoption took place not only in the context of isolated children being adopted into an existing family but also when children within a household came to full age so that they might "receive the full rights of sons" (Galatians 4:5, NIV). Until that event took place a child might indeed be the heir of the whole household, but until he was "adopted" or received the full rights of sonship he might appear like any other child in the household.

Imagine a guest seeing children playing together in the courtyard of a large Roman household. All the children, including brothers and sisters, slave children and others, look similar as they play their game together, but one is being pointed out as the heir of the whole household. While the children play together he looks like any other child. Indeed he lives like any other child under the authority of one of the slaves whose task is to be a child-minder. "The *paidagogos* was a slave charged with the supervision of a boy during his minority. He was responsible for his dress, food, speech and manners, and would accompany him to school. He was a disciplinarian and was allowed to administer corporal punishment, so that he was often depicted in ancient drawings as wielding a rod" (John Stott, *Calling Christian Leaders*, IVP, 2002).

The child has no authority while he is still a child, but when the day of adoption comes he is elevated, singled out and given full rights of sonship. Paul argues that in the coming of Christ, who himself fulfilled the law, a new day has dawned whereby you have obtained your full rights as an heir. Since you are now an heir, how could you ever return to subject yourself to the child-minder? Have you fully understood what God has done?

"Abba! Father!"

Paul takes the argument further by saying that not only have you received the rights of a son but "because you are sons, God has sent forth the Spirit of His Son into our hearts, crying 'Abba! Father!'" (Galatians 4:6) You now have your guarantee of sonship. The Holy Spirit bears witness with your spirit that you are a child of God. The New Covenant has begun and you have entered into a new relationship with God that surpasses the Old Testament believers' relationship with law. Life in the Spirit has come to replace life in subjection to the outward letter of the law. The heir no longer relates to the authority of the child-minder but enjoys new, direct, intimate access to his Father, aided by the indwelling Holy Spirit.

Because the law's role has been fulfilled in bringing you to Christ, it is of crucial importance that you don't go back to law, failing to grasp the new and glorious liberty into which you have been brought as a son and, indeed, an heir of God, with the inner witness of the Holy Spirit confirming the full rights of sonship.

You are not under law but under grace (Romans 6:14). You must never return to law as though your salvation were incomplete without it. You must revel in the gift of righteousness that the New Covenant provides. Paul was heartbroken about his contemporary Jews, that they were still trying to establish a righteousness of their own derived from the law, instead of embracing the gift of righteousness that comes from God on the basis of faith (see Philippians 3:9). In Romans he says similarly, "for not knowing about God's righteousness and seeking to establish their own, they did not subject themselves to the righteousness of God. For Christ is the *end of the law for righteousness* to everyone who believes" (Romans 10:3, 4 – italics mine).

You will never reign in life and be free from the clouds of condemnation if you do not wholeheartedly embrace the free gift of righteousness. You need to enjoy the glorious liberty of being a child of God, thoroughly accepted, not on the basis of your present performance as a law keeper but thoroughly on the basis of his gift of the righteousness of Christ fully reckoned to your account. You are fully accepted in the Beloved.

Strangely, adding law takes away from grace, distorts the gospel and leaves you confused and condemned. But, praise God, "there is now no condemnation for those who are in Christ Jesus" (Romans 8:1), a truth we must investigate in our next chapter.

3

The free gift of righteousness

How can you stand before a holy God and be thoroughly acceptable? Through the death and resurrection of Christ, God has found a way to justify freely those who believe. He gives you his perfect spotless righteousness as a gift. Jesus Christ is your righteousness and he is the same yesterday, today and forever.

In this chapter you will discover that you are no longer in Adam but in Christ, and that his obedience to his Father's will makes you righteous in God's sight.

The free gift of righteousness

We reign in life not only through the abundance of grace but also through the free gift of righteousness (Romans 5:17). Righteousness is a fundamental issue. The enjoying of God's grace flows from the certainty that you are accepted before him as righteous. You will always be vulnerable to Satan's pointed finger of accusation if you don't understand and wholeheartedly embrace the gift of righteousness that God has freely given you.

I shall never forget the first time God spoke to me through Zechariah chapter 3. Joshua the High Priest was standing before God and tragically, though he was High Priest, he was clothed in filthy garments, which thoroughly disqualified him from fulfilling his priestly role of worship. Satan was at hand to point out his failure and bring it to God's attention, something I was constantly aware of in my own experience. One can imagine Joshua wondering what his excuses might be or how he could plead his cause, but before he could say anything, God speaks, rebuking Satan and providing fresh clothing and a new mitre for his appointed priest to stand head erect in his presence. Satan's accusing mouth is closed!

God is the one who justifies

The story demonstrates the truth that Paul later develops in Romans 8, namely, "God is the one who justifies" (Romans 8:33). Before we can ever justify ourselves God steps in, provides a perfect righteousness and thoroughly and permanently justifies us. When feeling condemned we so often try to justify ourselves by looking at our current performance. We try to build up our own merit points by increasing our efforts at sanctification.

Sometimes this confusion is established from the very beginning of our conversion experience. Instead of hearing a clear proclamation of the New Covenant, some hear a mixture of Old and New Covenant concepts. Imagine the following scenario. You are a carefree individual, generally coping with life. Suddenly you find yourself working alongside a genuine born-again Christian whose consistent lifestyle of integrity, peace and friendliness provokes you to ask questions. Feeling a mixture of envy and personal failure as you compare your life with his, you pluck up courage to ask him why he is so different and he tells you that he is a Christian, and invites you to attend his church.

On arrival, you are surprised to find others like him who seem genuinely at peace and are clearly experiencing some kind of relationship with God that satisfies them and helps them in their lives. Your first reaction may well be to try to clean up your act, but you quickly discover your inability to change. As you continue attending church you feel a growing conviction of your sin.

One day the light is turned on. For the first time, you hear that Jesus Christ died for sinners and that you can come to God for forgiveness just as you are. All your sins can be washed away. You can know that God has accepted you. You can be assured of eternal life. You can come to God and invite him to come into your very life. Maybe you walk to the front of the meeting and invite Christ to be your Saviour. You are born again and your joy knows no bounds. This is what you have been looking for for years!

Then you are taken aside by the counsellor who wants to pass on some very important information, namely that now that you are a Christian, it is very important that you do certain things and refrain from others. You need to read your Bible every day. You need to spend a certain amount of time praying. You might like to consider changing the style of your clothing and maybe where you spend your time. The rules vary from place to place and church to church, but in reality many people on the day of their conversion meet with a mixture of freedom and implied bondage, the lightening of their load, quickly followed by the imposition of a new load. Yes, you have found freedom but you have also found a lot of new rules to live by. Sadly for many, they sense that their enjoyment of Christianity will have a lot to do with their ability to keep the rules. The new Christian quickly becomes acquainted with the burden of unworthiness and inadequacy.

In many churches this is very much the norm among existing Christians. Unless a church has been invaded by clear teaching on the grace of God it can often breathe an atmosphere that lacks joy and seems far removed from the ethos of the early church.

It's a gift!

If you are not thoroughly persuaded that God has given you a gift of righteousness that makes you thoroughly acceptable to God, you will constantly be battling with a general sense of disqualification and guilt. You will fear that you are not sanctified enough to be acceptable to God and this is where you will make a huge mistake. It is of crucial importance that you distinguish between sanctification and justification. Every Christian knows the battle with feelings of condemnation but it is of huge importance that you use the right weapons in the fight. If you try to resist feelings of unworthiness on the basis of your sanctification, you will never overcome the accusing finger of condemnation. God has provided you with a complete and adequate answer, which is not sanctification but justification.

God has justified you freely! He has given you thorough acceptance in his sight, not because of your changed life but because of his good pleasure in giving you the very righteousness of Christ. A breathtaking exchange has taken place. God has reconciled you through the death of his Son. "He made Him who knew no sin to be sin on our behalf, so that we might become the righteousness of God in Him" (2 Corinthians 5:21). The perfect, spotless righteousness of Jesus Christ has been accredited to your account. The righteousness of Christ is not an abstract concept. Jesus of Nazareth walked the earth and never sinned. He never asked his Father to forgive him. He never regretted a foolish word or a sinful act. He never had to say "sorry" to God or man. Daily, he lived a life of perfect choices, righteous acts and compassionate goodness. A thoroughly righteous life was lived on planet earth by a thoroughly righteous man and his righteousness has been completely credited to your account! He took your sin and gave you his righteousness.

The Old Testament prepared us for this concept with its instruction concerning the offering of unblemished lambs for sacrifice. The lamb to be offered had to be free from disease or blemish. Its limbs had to be perfect. When the worshipper brought his lamb for offering he did not fear that the priest might notice that he himself was badly dressed, that his clothes were torn or dirty. He was not at all self-conscious. All eyes were on the lamb. Would the priest find fault with the lamb? If the lamb was perfect, he was accepted.

Praise God, he has now provided a perfect lamb for us. Not only could Pilate find no fault with him. All heaven knew him to be innocent, undefiled and separate from sin. Because no fault can be found with our lamb we are thoroughly accepted.

It is said of John Bunyan, author of the renowned *Pilgrim's Progress*, that one day he was experiencing a season of depression. Walking and feeling dejected, he saw a vision of Jesus Christ. In that moment he comprehended that Jesus Christ was his righteousness. He understood in a new way that if he felt bright, robust and happy in God he could in no way actually add to the righteousness of Christ, nor could he, if he felt low or dejected, take away from the righteousness of Christ. Suddenly he understood with new certainty and joy that Jesus Christ was his righteousness and he's the same yesterday, today and forever.

Day by day you must arm yourself with this "breastplate of righteousness" (Ephesians 6:14), guarding your emotions from the fiery darts of the Devil. Because Jesus has cancelled all the handwriting that was against you and nailed it to his cross (see Colossians 2:14) he has thereby "disarmed the rulers and authorities" (Colossians 2:15). You overcome the accuser who accuses you day and night, by the blood of the Lamb and the word of your testimony and by not loving your own life unto death (see Revelation 12:10, 11). Satan's chief occupation against the believer, the weapon that he uses "day and night", is the weapon of accusation. If you don't know how to overcome his accusations your head will certainly go down. You will succumb to feelings of guilt and failure. You must stand securely clothed in the breastplate of righteousness and hold up the shield of faith that is perfectly adequate to withstand every fiery dart. Christ's unchanging righteousness is yours every day and is not in the least dependent on your feelings or your performance!

Although it should always be your desire to grow in grace and perfect your sanctification, you should never fight Satan's endeavours to condemn by arguing for your present sanctification. God's answer to condemnation is justification. You cannot be condemned and justified at the same time. If the judge declares you not guilty there is no condemnation, and the promise plainly declares that there is no condemnation for those who are in Christ Jesus (Romans 8:1). God has spoken. Your acceptance in Christ is beyond argument.

In Adam or in Christ

Paul's favourite title for a Christian is one who is "in Christ". Because of your relationship with Christ you obtain the benefits of all that Christ gained for you. Paul argues that the human race was essentially "in Adam" but those who put their trust in the Lord Jesus are regarded as no longer "in Adam" but rather "in Christ". The new relationship affords them wonderful benefits just as their old relationship with Adam was the root of their original problem. In Romans 5 Paul contrasts the results of being either in Adam or in Christ and actually sees Adam as a "type" of Christ. As Douglas Moo says, "The word 'type' denotes those Old Testament persons, institutions, or events that have a divinely intended function of prefiguring" (Douglas Moo, *The Epistle to the Romans*, NICNT, Eerdmans, 1996). Preachers often refer to Noah's ark as a "type" of Christ. You had to be in the ark to be saved. Some would argue that personalities such as Moses or David were types of Christ in their relationship with the people of God and their representative calling to serve God. They were like Christ in the task that they fulfilled and the person they represented. Joseph is often seen to be a "type" of Christ in his being rejected by his brothers, apparently dying only to be "alive from the dead" and established at the right hand of Pharaoh with all authority. Such Old Testament "types" shed light on the person and work of Christ.

It is strange, however, to regard Adam as a type of Christ since he was a sinner and failed God. In what way then does

Paul see Adam as a type of Christ? In Romans 5 Paul shows that Adam's sin corrupted the human race:

"... through one man sin entered into the world ..." (Romans 5:12)

"... by the transgression of the one, the many died ..." (Romans 5:15)

"... the judgment arose from one transgression, resulting in condemnation ..." (Romans 5:17)

"... by the transgression of the one, death reigns through the one ..." (Romans 5:17)

"... through one transgression there resulted condemnation to all men ..." (Romans 5:18)

"... through the one man's disobedience the many were made sinners ..." (Romans 5:19)

It is evident from Paul's argument that Adam's sin produced an unholy people. His disobedience is reckoned to our account. No amount of religious activity could remove this fundamental guilt. We were made sinners by Adam's sin. We are condemned through his guilt. We need to start life all over again. As Jesus said to Nicodemus, "That which is born of the flesh is flesh" (John 3:6). Jesus went on to argue, "Unless one is born again he cannot see the kingdom of God" (John 3:3), adding, "You must be born again" (John 3:7). You must get out of Adam into Christ. While you remain in Adam no amount of religious activity can save you. All your righteousness remains as filthy rags. All your endeavour to live a good life falls short of God's required standard and you are still blighted with your sin. It simply does not take you out of Adam and therefore leaves you guilty.

But Adam is a type of Christ. If your life was thoroughly blighted by your relationship with Adam, what contrasting gains do you make by being in Christ? Once you are in Christ you have been given his righteousness as a gift. Just as your sinfulness resulted from your relationship with

Adam, so now your righteousness comes from your new relationship with Jesus.

> ". . . so through one act of righteousness the result is justifica-
> tion of life to all men" (Romans 5:18)
> ". . . so through the obedience of the one the many will be
> made righteous" (Romans 5:19)

Now Christ is your righteousness. Just as when you were in Adam, your endeavours to live the holy life did not take you out of Adam and so left you as a sinner, so now you are in Christ and your sinful actions do not take you out of Christ but leave you still righteous in his sight. It is by virtue of your relationship with Jesus that you are thoroughly accepted. Your own personal failings do not take you out of him and therefore his righteousness still stands to your account.

The scandal of the gospel is that God is willing to justify the ungodly. "But to one who does not work, but believes in Him who justifies the ungodly, his faith is credited as righteousness" (Romans 4:5).

Enjoy your freedom

But isn't this a desperately dangerous doctrine? Does this not lead to carelessness? Does it not mean that you can carry on and live as you please but still be regarded as righteous? Isn't this a recipe for disaster? You might even ask the question, "What should we say then? Are we to continue in sin so that grace might increase?" And having asked that question, you might feel it has a familiar sound. Where have I heard that question before? Actually, you have heard it in Romans 6:1. Paul himself asks that very question because the gospel of grace is so free that it forces that question to the surface.

As Dr Martyn Lloyd-Jones said,

The true preaching of the gospel of salvation by grace alone always leads to the possibility of this charge being brought against it. There is no better test as to whether a man is really preaching the New Testament gospel of salvation than this, that some people might misunderstand it and misinterpret it to mean that it really amounts to this, that because you are saved by grace alone it does not matter at all what you do; you can go on sinning as much as you like because it will redound all the more to the glory of grace. That is a very good test of gospel preaching. If my preaching and presentation of the gospel of salvation does not expose it to that misunderstanding then it is not the gospel. If a man preaches justification by works, no one would ever raise this question." (D Martyn Lloyd-Jones, *Romans: The New Man, An Exposition of Chapter 6,* Banner of Truth Trust, 1972)

The gospel of grace raises the question that if righteousness is so free, shall we not carry on sinning as before? In stark contrast, the message of legalism will never prompt that question. The gospel of grace is a message of breathtaking freedom. It must be embraced with faith and thanksgiving. You are thoroughly accepted just as you are. Jesus Christ is your righteousness and he is never going to change. He is the same yesterday, today and forever. When you wake tomorrow, he will still be your righteousness, before you have done anything to deserve God's favour. You have to earn nothing. Your spirit needs to bask in the brilliant sunlight of this reality. You need to know it inwardly and celebrate it on a daily basis.

Because it is so free, many preachers, fearful of antinomianism (i.e. lawlessness) and a careless attitude to sin, are quick to add cautionary riders that obscure the message. It is better to pause before adding anything or even before pressing on into Romans 6. If you muddle the teaching of Romans 5 by rushing on quickly to Romans 6 you can blur the message. If you confuse justification with sanctification you are in trouble.

When I was a schoolboy, I occasionally did watercolour painting. When painting a landscape, we were taught to begin with a light blue wash from the top of the page. We were then told to leave it to dry. The temptation was not to wait but to press on and paint the rest of the picture, to add hills and trees, before the blue sky had dried. The problem was that, if you did not wait for the paint to dry but added green hills and brown trees, you did not actually create a beautiful picture but a terrible mess, as one wet colour merged into another on the page.

It was imperative to let the colour dry. Then you could add other things and complete the picture. So it is with the message of grace. Let it dry! Don't add to it too quickly; let the wonder of God's grace overwhelm you. Let his grace set you free. Let it bring you into a deep sense of his total acceptance of you, just as you are!

4

Shall we carry on sinning?

It is one thing to know that you are forgiven, but how do you get free from the power of sin and from past habits and thought patterns that have dominated your life?

Jesus promised that the truth would set you free, and the truth is that you have died to your bondage to sin; you have died with Christ and been raised with him. Knowing the truth is crucial to your freedom. Applying the truth with faith and responsibility will bring you into a place of joyful liberty.

Shall we carry on sinning?

I was once preaching a message on the grace of God when a man in the congregation stood to interrupt me. "I have never heard anything so outrageous in all my life!" he complained. The scandal of the gospel of grace had so offended him that he could not stay silent.

To be honest, I was rather thrilled at his reaction and respectfully asked him to sit, adding that he had *almost* understood everything I was saying and that if he would wait to hear the whole message I was sure he would be happy. Half the message of God's grace can alarm sober Christians and sound totally irresponsible.

Having concluded his teaching on Romans 5, Paul certainly felt the need to pose the question of Romans 6:1, "What shall we say then? Are we to continue in sin so that grace might increase?" followed by his heartfelt response, "May it never be!" (Romans 6:2), or as J B Phillips translates it, "What a ghastly thought!" (J B Phillips, *Letters to Young Churches*, Fontana, 1947).

The fact is that one rarely hears Christians asking such a question – or at least not in public! More often, one hears a question that sounds like the flip side of that same coin. It goes something like this, "I know that God has accepted me. I know I am saved, but how can I actually be freed from the power of sin?"

It could be illustrated by reference to the Israelites at the time of the exodus. They knew they had escaped the night of God's judgement through trusting in the blood of the Passover lambs on their doorposts. Judgement had passed over and they were safe, redeemed by the blood of an unblemished lamb.

Notice incidentally that the blood was to be placed on the *outside of their houses*. The blood was for *God* to see, not for their benefit. The blood was not to make them feel good or feel safe. The blood was not for their feelings at all. The blood was to satisfy God. It was for his eyes alone, just as later the blood of atonement would be offered in the Holy of Holies where no other man was present. God said, "When I see the blood I will pass over you" (Exodus 12:13). We have peace, not because we feel good, but because God is satisfied with the blood. Only he can evaluate the worth of the blood of the lamb. Because he is satisfied, we have peace.

There would have been no point in the Israelites repeatedly opening the door in order to gaze on the blood to see if they felt any better or more acceptable or worthy. On that night the blood was efficacious. In every Egyptian home, the firstborn died. In every Hebrew home the blood of the lamb covered them.

Having been delivered from judgement, however, the Israelites found their way obstructed by the Red Sea. As the Egyptians pursued, they became increasingly aware that although they had been "passed over" by God, they were still captive in the land of slavery. They were not free at all! Many Christians feel like that: forgiven but still slaves, accepted but not free from bondage to all kinds of sins and habits that still seem to dominate their lives.

In Romans 6 Paul tells us the secret of the glorious liberty that Jesus has won for us. Just as the Israelites were actually freed from slavery by going down into the Red Sea valley and out the other side, so those who are in Christ have been delivered from the power of sin so that they can live a life of overcoming. As Paul confidently proclaims in Romans 6:14, "Sin shall not be master over you, for you are not under law but under grace."

Notice the step-by-step process that Paul opens up to his readers. Perhaps I should first point out what Paul does not say. He does not say that your problem is that you are trying too hard. You just need to stop striving and relax. All you need is to "let go and let God". Let Jesus do it in you. Simply hand it all over to God. Simply come to the front of the meeting and surrender your will to the Lord. These kinds of suggestions are frequently offered to people who long to grow in God, but sadly they are in stark contrast to the apostle Paul's plain teaching.

Knowing the truth sets you free

Paul presents three straightforward steps. First, he wants you to *know* some things. Jesus said, "You will know the truth, and the truth will set you free" (John 8:32). Knowing truth is essential for your growth in God.

Paul wants to make sure that you know what was accomplished for you through the death of Christ. "Do you not know that all of us who have been baptised into Christ Jesus have been baptised into his death?" (Romans 6:3). He asks the question, "How shall we who died to sin still live in it?" (Romans 6:2).

The truth is that all who are in Christ have "died to sin". Notice that Paul is not talking about some elite Christians who have had a remarkable extra blessing and have actually died to sin and its power. Paul is not talking about *some* of us but *all* of us. This is true of all who are in Christ. There are not three categories: first, those who are in Adam; second, those who are in Christ; and third, those special

Christians who are in Christ and have actually died to sin. Paul is talking about all who are in Christ.

Notice also that he is not speaking of a future experience which offers you freedom and which he would like you to seek after. He is speaking of something in the past tense that has already happened to all who are in Christ. He restates the truth slightly differently in verse 6: "Knowing this, that our old self was crucified with him, in order that our body of sin might be done away with, in order that we would no longer be slaves to sin", adding in verse 7, "He who has died is freed from sin."

Did you know that your old self was crucified with Christ and that you are no longer a slave of sin? This is truth you need to know! The gospel is good news! You might argue, "I don't feel very freed from sin", or "My old self doesn't feel very crucified with Christ." This is where you must allow the truth to have full authority in your thoughts. Will you believe what God says is true or do you consistently yield to your feelings? Perhaps it would help if I asked another question. Do you believe that at Calvary two men were crucified with Christ, one on the right and one on the left? Why do you believe that? Because the Bible says so. Now you have the same authority for believing that your old self was crucified with him. The Bible says so!

How you see yourself is vitally important. When the Israelites came to the Promised Land we are told that they saw themselves as grasshoppers (Numbers 13:31–33) and, therefore, incapable of inheriting it. God was far from pleased with their assessment and the unbelief that kept them from entering in.

I remember as a young Christian being shocked to find myself apparently gripped with jealousy towards a certain fellow Christian in the young people's group at my church. I was plagued with a terrible attitude towards this person. One day I was actually on my daily train journey to work in London when I was reading this passage in Romans 6.

Suddenly the truth hit me with tremendous impact. My old self was crucified with Christ and "he who has died is freed from sin" (Romans 6:7). Dead people don't feel jealous. Dead people don't get upset if someone else is praised. Dead people are free! It came home to me with such force that I laughed out loud in the train compartment. I remember people staring at me. No doubt they thought, "Funny guy, not only reads the Bible but laughs at it too!" But the fact is that the truth had set me free and we enjoyed an excellent relationship from that time on.

If God declares that you are free, you are free! As J B Phillips translates Romans 6:7, "Let us never forget that our old selves died with Him on the cross, that the tyranny of sin over us might be broken – for a dead man can safely be said to be immune to the power of sin" (J B Phillips, *Letters to Young Churches*, Fontana, 1947). As men and women of faith, you are called upon to agree with God, like Abraham who did not waver through unbelief regarding the promise of God but was strengthened in his faith, giving glory to God, and being fully assured that what God had promised he was able also to perform (see Romans 4:20–21).

Count yourself dead to sin

Having reminded you of things you need to know, Paul takes you to a second step, namely that you are to *consider* yourself to be dead to sin (Romans 6:11). As the New International Version translates it, *count* yourself dead to sin. The word translated "reckon" or "consider" or "count" is actually borrowed from the world of accountancy and carries the meaning of making sure that you have things in the right column. You are to consider yourself dead to sin, not in order to make it happen but because you know it has already happened. This is not "mind over matter" or the power of positive thinking. Paul is not telling you that if you think about it hard enough you will make it become true. He is saying that because it is true, you must make sure you consider it true and not allow your mind to slip back into your former mindset.

Let me illustrate. You might find yourself arriving from London at Barcelona airport. The captain informs you that the time is now 4 p.m. You look at your watch and clearly it says 3 p.m. You have a good watch and it's still working. Why should the pilot say that it is 4 p.m. when your watch clearly tells you that it is 3 p.m.? How do you proceed? Do you keep him happy by pretending that you agree that it is 4 p.m. when you really know full well that it is actually 3 p.m.? Should you try hard to consider that it is 4 p.m.? No. The reality is that in Spain it is 4 p.m. Spain is in a different time zone to England. They are one hour ahead, so you change your watch and line up with Spain. Similarly, you are now in Christ and therefore dead to sin. You are living in a different location, so change your thinking! When you move to a different time zone you change your watch. When you move from Adam into Christ you shift into a new life where you can count yourself dead to sin, because God says you are.

Take responsibility

Paul now tells you the third step you must take: "Therefore do not let sin reign in your mortal body so that you obey its lusts and do not go on presenting the members of your body to sin as instruments of unrighteousness" (Romans 6:12, 13). Sin is looking for somewhere to reign and Paul tells you not to let it reign in your mortal body.

Why do you suppose he uses the word "mortal"? Why does he not simply tell you not to let sin reign in your body? Perhaps he uses the word "mortal" to remind us that our body will ultimately die – it is not immortal. Although you have passed from death to everlasting life your body has not yet been saved. "We ourselves groan within ourselves, waiting eagerly for our adoption as sons, the redemption of our body" (Romans 8:23). Our bodies have yet to be redeemed. "We eagerly wait for a Saviour, the Lord Jesus Christ, who will transform the body of our humble state into conformity with the body of his glory" (Philippians 3:20–21). Until we get our new bodies "we have this treasure in earthen vessels" (2 Corinthians 4:7). So you have been transformed and redeemed but your body has not. In the past, when you were in slavery to sin, your sin was mostly expressed through your body and its members. Now Paul gives you the instruction no longer to allow sin to reign in your body and no longer to yield your members as instruments of sin. Like a musician, sin is looking for an instrument. It cannot "make music" without an instrument. As a renewed person, you are to take authority over your body and its members and refuse to allow sin to reign there.

Before you were saved, your old self and your body were in happy agreement to sin. Now, as one who has been freed from sin, you must take absolute authority over your body and its members. Hands, eyes, tongue, lips and ears, all used to serve sin; they must now serve the new life that is in you. As a new man, you must make wise choices about where you spend your time, what you read, where you allow your eyes to gaze, and what you permit your hands to touch. You are no longer a slave of sin. You must live out your liberty.

Indeed, Paul makes a number of categorical statements. "Sin shall not be master over you" (Romans 6:14). He acknowledges that "you *were* slaves of sin" (Romans 6:17) but now you are in a new place: "Having been freed from sin, you became slaves of righteousness" (Romans 6:18). Paul makes a wonderful announcement that, whereas once you were sin's slave, you have now become "slaves of righteousness". Once again it is important to notice the tense that Paul uses. This is something that has happened to you. You used to be sin's slave, at his beck and call, without freedom of choice, owned and dominated by sin. Now you have become the slave of righteousness. You are in bondage to righteousness. Righteousness dominates your life and directs your days. You have been purchased at the slave market. You are no longer sin's slave but belong to a new master. You have a new identity and a new owner. Your responsibility is to yield yourself and your members on a daily basis to this new master. As Jesus said, "If the Son sets you free you will be free indeed" (John 8:36).

Moses did not lead the Israelites only to the Passover but right through the Red Sea and out into freedom from slavery. Similarly, Christians are not only covered by the blood of Christ, their Passover (1 Corinthians 5:7), but have been freed from slavery, no longer in bondage to the power of sin. Grace does a thorough job. The grace of God gets you out of sin; it doesn't encourage you to remain in it. "Sin shall not be master over you, for you are not under law but under grace" (Romans 6:14).

As Douglas Moo comments on this verse, "The paragraph that began with the question 'should we remain in sin that grace might increase?' ends with the glad tidings that we are under grace that sin might be overcome" (Douglas Moo, *The Epistle to the Romans*, NICNT, Eerdmans, 1996).

God has not called us to a life of slavery but to one of overcoming.

5

Are you free or not?

Are we really free? Didn't Paul acknowledge in Romans 7 that in reality he was secretly in terrible bondage to sin? He preached to others, but didn't he own up to having personal problems just like the rest of us?

It is very important that we understand Romans 7. In this chapter we shall look carefully at the arguments and quote a number of scholars who argue both that the gospel really does set you free and that Romans 7 is not meant to confuse or disappoint you, but rather to underline the impotence of the law to save or sanctify.

Are you free or not?

Probably no other chapter in the New Testament is the basis for more debate than Romans 7. Paul, having declared your freedom in such graphic and uncompromising terms in chapter 6, makes statements in chapter 7 that, at first glance, seem thoroughly to contradict what he has just unequivocally proclaimed.

In chapter 6 he has said:

"How shall we who died to sin still live in it?" (Romans 6:2)
"Our old self was crucified with Him . . . that we would no
   longer be slaves to sin" (Romans 6:6)
"He that has died is freed from sin" (Romans 6:7)
"Consider yourselves to be dead to sin" (Romans 6:11)
"Do not let sin reign in your mortal body" (Romans 6:12)
"Sin shall not be master over you" (Romans 6:14)
"Having been freed from sin, you became slaves of righteous-
   ness" (Romans 6:18)

Not only does chapter 6 repeatedly declare your freedom, chapter 8 continues in the same vein by telling you, "Therefore, there is now no condemnation for those who are in Christ Jesus" (Romans 8:1) and continues by telling you that "the law of the Spirit of life in Christ Jesus has set you free from the law of sin and death" (Romans 8:2).

So what does Paul mean when, in chapter 7, he says such things as:

"I am of the flesh, sold into bondage to sin" (Romans 7:14)
"I know that nothing good dwells in me" (Romans 7:18)
"The good that I want, I do not do, but practise the very evil that I do not want" (Romans 7:19)
"Wretched man that I am, who will set me free from the body of this death?" (Romans 7:24)

Godly teachers throughout the generations have differed in their interpretation of this passage, so it is certainly appropriate to approach the passage with respect and caution. Certainly, we do not have space here thoroughly to research every point that could be made, but I must acknowledge indebtedness to a number of respected scholars.

First, I know that I have been deeply impressed by the arguments raised by Dr Martyn Lloyd-Jones (D Martyn Lloyd-Jones, *The Law, Romans 7:1 – 8:4,* Banner of Truth Trust, 1973) in which he makes the strong case that throughout Romans, Paul has been dealing with the vital matter of justification by faith and God's willingness to give the gift of righteousness to the believer in spite of his own actual condition (e.g. Romans 4:4–5).

Dr Lloyd-Jones argues that Paul's teaching on God's amazing grace raises huge questions in the mind of the reader, two in particular. First, if God is prepared to call us righteous shall we simply carry on sinning? Paul answers this in chapter 6, as we have seen. The second question that arises is, what about the place of the law? If God is prepared to accept us by virtue of our faith in Christ, where does the law fit into the picture? Chapter 7 answers this question. Dr Lloyd-Jones teaches that it is essentially a chapter about the law, not a chapter telling us Paul's personal testimony.

As Thomas Schreiner says, "My own view is that Paul's purpose in the text is not to delineate whether believers or unbelievers are the subject of the discussion. His purpose is to communicate the inability of the law to transform human beings" (Thomas R Schreiner, *Paul, Apostle of God's Glory in Christ*, IVP, 2001). Having answered the question about the law, Paul returns to his theme in Romans 8, which follows on very well from the conclusion of Romans 5, after the two parenthetical chapters.

Some have suggested an alternative view, that the Christian has, as it were, to experientially work his way out of Romans 7 into Romans 8. They point out that Romans 7 makes no reference to the Holy Spirit, and add that the inner conflict of Romans 7 is resolved when one personally experiences the Holy Spirit (mentioned in Romans 8) and emerges free. But this teaching ignores the glorious freedom already proclaimed in Romans 5 and 6, and embraces a false concept that Romans 7 to 8 is a journey that individual Christians have to take.

Can this really be Paul's Christian testimony?

Another point made by Dr Lloyd-Jones that greatly impacted me is the actual weight and seriousness of the words used. Paul does not simply say that he is aware of experiencing some difficult days in his Christian life, or that sometimes he is conscious of inner conflict, statements that perhaps many Christians could identify with. Paul appears to confess far more and makes very dramatic statements, namely, that he is in bondage to sin (verse 14), that nothing good dwells in him (verse 18), that he practises the evil that he does not want to (verse 19), and that he is a wretched man, not knowing where to turn for deliverance (verse 24).

Can this really be understood to be Paul's testimony? Was he really *in bondage* to sin? Did *nothing* good dwell in him? Did he continually practise unwanted evil? If this is indeed the secret of his inner life, why does he so confidently urge others to imitate him and follow his example (into bondage and wretchedness)? How can he so repeatedly testify to his own inner joy, peace and contentment? Also, why is there no other passage in Paul's letters, or indeed in any other New Testament writers' epistles, that in any way parallels Paul's dramatic statements here? Peter, for instance, tells us, "His divine power has given us everything we need for life and godliness" (2 Peter 1:3, NIV). John adds, "No one who lives in him keeps on sinning. No one who continues to sin has either seen him or known him" (1 John 3:6, NIV). Paul confidently tells the Corinthians, "No temptation has overtaken you but such as is common to man; and God is faithful, who will not allow you to be tempted beyond what you are able, but with the temptation will provide the way of escape also, so that you will be able to endure it" (1 Corinthians 10:13).

Elsewhere, Paul testifies that he is "conscious of nothing against himself" (1 Corinthians 4:4). This does not sound like the troubled soul on display in Romans 7. In 1 Corinthians 4:3, he claims not to be particularly preoccupied with self-examination, "In fact, I do not even examine myself." This must be balanced by his other words in the same epistle in connection with the celebration of the Lord's Supper where he says, "A man must examine himself" (1 Corinthians 11:28). Clearly, we are not to lack self-inspection but the overall impact of Paul's words seems to suggest that he is not overly preoccupied with self-examination.

Another verse that sheds light is found in 1 Corinthians 6:12 where he says, "All things are lawful to me, but not all things are profitable. All things are lawful for me, but I will not be mastered by anything." How can we compare this confident assertion, "I will not be mastered by anything", with his apparently helpless confession in Romans 7, "The good that I want to do, I do not do, but practise the very evil that I do not want"? Or with his question, "Who will set me free?" This sounds like a man thoroughly mastered! It simply does not add up.

Certainly, the Christian life is a call to fight the good fight of faith. It requires your being strong in the Lord and in the strength of his might and taking the whole armour of God. But nowhere else is it seen as the hopeless cry of a wretched captive.

God is at work in you to will and to do

Certainly, you must work out your salvation with fear and trembling (Philippians 2:12), but notice you do so with the promise that "God is at work in you both to will and to work for His good pleasure" (Philippians 2:13). What a clear contrast to the Romans 7 man who testifies that "the willing is present with me, but the doing of the good is not" (Romans 7:18)! Paul is conscious that God is at work in him in both the "willing" and the "doing", unlike the wretched Romans 7 figure who "wills" but finds no power to "do", nor knows how to get free from his wretchedness! What kind of a Christian is this? Is it really Paul's testimony?

As Gordon Fee helpfully argues,

> Christian ethics lies not just in the "willing." In Rom 7:18, in his description of life before and outside of Christ, but looked at from the perspective of life in the Spirit, Paul described *pre-Christian life* with these same verbs. To "will," he said, was present with me; he recognized the good and spiritual thing that the Law truly is. But without the Spirit, he goes on, "carrying out the good" does not happen. As a believer, however, Paul will have none of that (i.e., of their not being able to carry out the good that they will); hence he urges the Philippians to "work it out" precisely because God (by his Spirit, is implied) is present with them both to will and to do "the good". (Gordon D Fee, *Paul's Letter to the Philippians*, NICNT, Eerdmans, 1995)

Richard Hays adds,

> The fundamental force of Paul's claim must not be missed: God
> is present in power in the church, changing lives and enabling
> an obedience that would otherwise be unattainable . . . The
> Holy Spirit is not a theological abstraction but the manifesta-
> tion of God's presence in the community, making everything
> new. Those who respond to the gospel have entered the sphere
> of the Spirit's power, where they find themselves changed and
> empowered for obedience. (Richard B Hays, *The Moral Vision
> of the New Testament*, T & T Clark, 1997)

As Douglas Moo argues,

> In chapter 6 and 8 respectively Paul makes it clear that "being
> free from under sin" and "being free from the law of sin and
> death" are conditions that are true for every Christian. If one
> is a Christian, then these things are true; if one is not, then they
> are not true. This means that the situation depicted in Romans
> 7:14–25 cannot be that of the "normal" Christian, nor of an
> immature Christian. (Douglas Moo, *The Epistle to the Romans*,
> NICNT, Eerdmans, 1996)

Having made this case, we cannot help asking whom Paul
is speaking about. Who is the person having this terrible
battle? It is argued that it cannot be the typical unbeliever
since he has none of the desires for holiness that the verses
describe. The sinner is indifferent to God and to righteousness. He has no great appetite for doing good.

Different views have been raised by different authors. Dr
Martyn Lloyd-Jones sees it as a description of the awakened
sinner who is not yet saved but has come under powerful
conviction of sin and is grappling with law-keeping as his
hoped-for way of salvation, only to meet with the corruption of his own nature and the inability of the law to save.

Douglas Moo argues that most likely it is a reference to

corporate Israel and that Paul is referring to himself "in solidarity with the Jewish people and therefore with the experience of the coming of the law at Sinai". He adds, "The experience of Israel with the law should also remind Christians never to return to the law – whether the Mosaic or any other list of 'rules' – as a source of spiritual vigour or growth" (Douglas Moo, *The Epistle to the Romans*, NICNT, Eerdmans, 1996).

Richard Hays says, "The agonized struggle of Romans 7 is hardly offered by Paul as a normative account of Christian experience. Rather, it is an account of existence 'in Adam' or under the Law or both" (Richard B Hays, *The Moral Vision of the New Testament*, T & T Clark, 1997).

Gordon Fee argues that "Paul is here describing life before and outside of Christ, but from the perspective of one who is himself now in Christ" (Gordon D Fee, *God's Empowering Presence*, Hendrickson, 1994).

N T Wright also teaches that what is driving Paul's argument is not his personal experience, but the question of whether the law itself is evil (N T Wright, *The Climax of the Covenant*, T & T Clark, 1991).

This must suffice for now. It is my conviction that Paul proclaims that the believer is freed from slavery to sin and that his teaching in Romans 7 in no way undermines that promise. The Christian is undoubtedly exhorted to win the ongoing battle with the world, the flesh and the Devil, but he is not to enter that battle fearing inevitable defeat and thinking that somehow the apostle Paul was also a defeated wretch.

Jesus promised, "So if the Son sets you free, you will be free indeed" (John 8:36). Commenting on this verse, D A Carson says,

Jesus not only enjoys inalienable rights as the unique Son of God, but exercises full authority vested in him by the Father to liberate slaves. Those whom Jesus liberates from the tyranny of sin are really (*ontos*) free. True freedom is not the liberty to do anything we please, but the liberty to do what we ought; and it is genuine liberty because doing what we ought now pleases us. (D A Carson, *The Gospel According to John*, Eerdmans, 1991)

So let me encourage you not to see Romans 7 as a discouraging setback, but to enjoy your freedom and take advantage of the mighty deliverance that Jesus obtained for you at such great cost.

6

A conscience cleansed from dead works

Grace sets you free from mere religious duty and routine. The freedom from condemnation obtained by Christ's blood cleanses and releases your conscience. You no longer have to prove your worth by being a busy Christian.

In this chapter we shall see that this freedom does not lead to indolence and indifference but clears the ground for zealous service for God's glory and for you to receive the reward of his "Well done good and faithful servant".

A conscience cleansed from dead works

Grace not only frees you from sin, guilt and disqualification, it also frees you from merely going through the motions and doing your religious duty. What do I mean? Perhaps it's best expressed in Hebrews 9:14 which tells us that the blood of Christ "cleanses your conscience from dead works to serve the living God". You have no need to get involved in what the Bible calls "dead works" (NIV margin – "religious rituals"). Most evangelical Christians would tend to think that they are already free from "dead religion". They associate such rituals with more formal church life of the "bells and smells" variety. As born-again Christians, they reckon that they have turned their backs on dead works.

Perhaps we should be more self-critical. What is a dead work? Inevitably, it is something which has no life in it, for instance something done without faith. Church life can easily become a matter of routine, demanding little or no faith. Sadly, routine can gradually rule the programme. We can find ourselves involved in activities, services and programmes that may have long since lost their purpose. No one actually remembers why we do them, but we still do.

A young woman once told me that she had asked her

mother why, when cooking the Sunday lunch, she always cut off the two ends of the roasting joint and placed them on the top. Her mother replied that she had no idea and supposed that it was in order that the juices might flow. She told her that Grandma had always done it. Perhaps she should ask Grandma. When my friend asked her grandmother, she looked at her granddaughter in astonishment. "Why are you still doing that?" she asked. "I used to do it when our oven was so small that it was the only way I could get the meat in."

Dull routine

Church programmes can be littered with events that have long since lost their raison d'être. We go through routines devoid of faith and expectation. Sometimes, churches hold Sunday evening "gospel services" which have not seen conversions for years. Unsaved people never attend. It is obviously not producing fruit. But still the service takes place. We lack the pragmatic ruthlessness that Jesus demonstrated when he encountered the fruitless fig tree. His instruction was simple and straightforward: "Cut it down!" When the disciples defended the tree, Jesus conceded that it could be tended for one more year, but if it then remained fruitless it should be axed. It was taking up space.

Mere church attendance that is not mixed with faith can soon become a dead work. What do we expect to happen when we meet? Why are we gathering? Has it become a duty that we perform?

Another kind of dead work to be avoided is one done presumptuously. Perhaps this is best illustrated by Joshua's experience at Jericho and what followed. The battle of Jericho was a famous act of faith. Thoroughly dependent upon God, Joshua followed instructions, marched his army around the city and gave the victory shout. Down came the walls and the city was taken – a phenomenal victory. What happened next?

Joshua asked about the next city. The report came back that Ai was a small place. A whole army wasn't needed. If they could defeat Jericho, Ai was a snip. A small army was sent, but instead of recording another great victory they were summarily defeated and dismissed, their tails between their legs. Joshua's army moved from a work of faith to a work of presumption in one easy step and learned a sad and painful lesson. God was not with them. It was a dead work.

Did God tell you to do it?

We must also beware of uncommanded work. A work that is not from God is a dead work, however good it looks. A door seems to open or a need presents itself. Someone ought to step in. As a young pastor, I was invited by my former school, in a nearby town, to teach religious education for one day a week. What an opportunity! I was particularly excited because my testimony at school had been ineffective and sporadic, at best. Now I could recover some of the lost ground and have some impact on the hundreds of students there.

As I thanked God in prayer for this wonderful opening, I felt that heaven was far less enthusiastic about this amazing door of opportunity than I was! Eventually, I felt that God asked me what he had called me to do. "Pastor this church, Lord" was my simple reply. "But thank you also for this wonderful open door into my old school." Again, silence from heaven. Gradually, I got it into my thick skull that God was not requiring me to go through this particular door. I called a friend who followed up the opening. It was an important lesson for me. Not all opportunities for Christian service are automatically for you.

Finally, in 1 Corinthians 13, Paul gives us a list of spiritual activities which seem to be unquestionably virtuous. He speaks of faith to move mountains, wisdom to fathom all mysteries, and the generosity to give all your possessions to the poor. But then he adds that you can do all these things without love and find that they are worthless and that you gain nothing. Works that are not motivated by love are unacceptable to God; they are mere religious activity.

The blood of Christ cleanses your conscience

The question arises, "Why do Christians get involved in dead works?" Our opening verse provides the key. It speaks of the blood of Christ cleansing your *conscience* from dead works. It seems that we can become very involved in dead works when we don't have a clear conscience and are insecure in the grace of God. If you are not sure of your acceptance and your freedom from condemnation you will be tempted to increase your performance to justify yourself before God and men. You do things so that you can feel better. You have not allowed the blood of Christ to do a thorough job on your conscience so that you know that it is cleansed in God's sight. As a result, you keep labouring to shake off feelings of failure and condemnation.

You need a clear understanding of Paul's breathtaking statement in Romans 4:4-5, "Now to the one who works his wage is not reckoned as a favour, but as what is due. But to the one who *does not work*, but who believes in him who justifies the ungodly, his faith is reckoned as righteousness" (my italics). Once you are utterly secure in that truth you can enjoy your freedom. You don't have to justify yourself. You don't have to impress others. You don't even have to impress God. In putting all your trust in Jesus and his cross you are saying that you have found one who has already impressed God on your behalf!

Indeed, if you have not come to rest in the finished work of the cross, but behave as though you can earn God's approval by personal performance, you are by implication saying that the cross is not enough. You need to add your own religious activity to be sure of his acceptance. The fact is that you cannot add to Christ's finished work. You need to repent of your dead works (Hebrews 6:1) and celebrate the fact that you are totally accepted! When your conscience is cleansed by the blood of Jesus, you will no longer be vulnerable to conscience-work. You must come to rest with the fact that God's blessing does not depend on your performance.

As a young pastor, working at the church I previously mentioned, I had spent some years being somewhat preoccupied with our own church and getting our own house in order. A time arrived when I felt that it would be appropriate to seek out more fellowship with other churches in the town. I approached the local ministers' fraternal and was warmly received. As a church, we were happy that a new phase of wider fellowship had started. A few days later, a gentleman arrived at my front door expressing his pleasure that we were now to be more involved with the local churches. He went on to say that in the following few weeks all of the churches would be delivering envelopes throughout the town asking for money and that at a later date the envelopes were to be collected. He was so pleased that we were now working with the churches and anticipated our enthusiastic involvement,

Sadly, I felt no sense that this was something that God would have us to do. I told the man that I was sorry but we would not be joining in. He expressed real surprise and said that he thought we were going to be involved from now on with all the churches. "All the other churches join in," he said, trying to unsettle my conscience and adding with a final twist of the knife, "even the Roman Catholics!" Because I was secure in my standing before God, I was untroubled by this attack on my conscience and stood my ground. I would not do what he wanted but still stood accepted by God with no need of self-justification. He could not manipulate me through guilt.

I wonder if you have ever become involved in Christian activity because of guilt manipulation: "Somebody needs to do it", or "We really need helpers, won't you get involved?" Many people buckle under the fear of what others will think of them and begin to get involved in activity for which they have neither faith nor love.

It is of crucial importance that you are free to say "No", secure in the knowledge that you are still righteous before God and don't have to do anything to justify your existence; grace sets you free!

You might ask, but if grace so pervades a church, will any work ever get done? Will people so celebrate their glorious freedom that they will never even consider doing any good works? Having discovered the grace of God will they become idle Christians for the rest of their lives?

Serving the living God

In answering the question, let me remind you of our opening verse, "The blood of Jesus cleanses your conscience from dead works to *serve the living God*" (my italics). It would appear that the living God expects to be served! You may not be called to dead works, but you are certainly called to serve. Titus 2:14 says that Jesus is seeking a people "zealous for good deeds". Jesus said, "Let your light shine before men in such a way that they may see your good works, and glorify your Father who is in heaven" (Matthew 5:16). He also added a note of urgency when he said, "We must work the works of Him who sent me, as long as it is day; night is coming, when no man can work" (John 9:4). Finally, the Bible records in its last chapter the words of Jesus, "Behold, I am coming quickly, and my reward is with me, to render to every man according to what he has done" (Revelation 22:12). It would appear from these verses that God is very interested in your works. He calls you to work in such a way that will bring glory to him and in such a way that he is able to reward you when Jesus returns.

You might ask where the subject of rewards fits in to the theme of grace? Few Christians ever consider the Bible's teaching on rewards, in spite of frequent references. Perhaps the most developed section in Paul's writings comes in 1 Corinthians 3 where Paul speaks of our works being tested by fire and the works that survive the fire test receiving a reward.

There are several factors in that passage to note. First, "Each man's work will become evident; for the day will show it because it is to be revealed with fire, and the fire itself will test the quality of each man's work" (1 Corinthians 3:13). There will be a meticulous inspection of every man's work. Each of us will give account to God for our works and the quality of the work will be examined by fire. Perhaps the example of our Lord Jesus sheds light on the theme. We are told, "He sat down opposite the treasury, and began observing how the multitude were putting money into the treasury" (Mark 12:41). Unlike the average pastor who might avert his gaze when people actually put their very private gifts into the offering, our Lord Jesus deliberately observed not only the actual gift, but what lay behind it in terms of motivation and resourcefulness. It is as though Jesus commanded the fire to fall upon the gifts that were given. "Rich people were putting in large sums. A poor widow came and put in two small copper coins" (Mark 12:41, 42). Jesus gives us an example of the personal assessment that every one of us is going to face one day. Imagine the fire falling and subsequently the smoke lifting to reveal what remained of the gifts of the rich people and the poor widow. The rich have lost their reward in the intensity of the flames, while the widow woman receives praise and honour from Jesus. "If any man's work . . . remains, he will receive a reward. If any man's work is burnt up, he will suffer loss; though he himself will be saved, yet so as through fire" (1 Corinthians 3:14, 15).

Have you ever faced the possibility of "suffering loss"? Paul makes it clear that we all face this possibility, though he is careful to add that we ourselves will be saved because we are, of course, saved by grace. We are thoroughly accepted because of the grace of God but our works will be given close scrutiny to see if they survive the fire test.

Each man's praise will come to him from God

What is Paul's own response to this prospect? He tells us that, because of the anticipated coming judgement, we should stop judging one another in a superficial way. He tells his readers that "to me it is a very small thing that I may be examined by you" (1 Corinthians 4:3). He is more aware of the reality that the Lord is coming "who will both bring to light the things hidden in the darkness and disclose the motives of men's hearts; then each man's praise will come to him from God" (1 Corinthians 4:5). A very searching examination will one day face every one of us. At that time, things hidden in the darkness will be brought to light. The motives of your heart will be made public. God is interested not only in your doing good deeds, he is also painstakingly interested in your motivations for doing them. The fire will test the purity of your motivations, so turn your back on dead works. They won't stand the fire test. God not only wants you to serve him, he wants you to do it for the right reason. Hence the church at Ephesus was challenged by the Lord Jesus because they lost their first love and were merely active. He warned them of church closure and the removal of their lampstand (Revelation 2:4–5). Jesus cannot cope with mere externalism and dull routine. The Laodicean church was similarly challenged because of its lukewarm approach (Revelation 3:15–16).

Having cleared the decks from the debris of dead works, ask yourself, how do I serve the living God? As a starting point, don't be dismissive of the subject of rewards. Many

Christians seem indifferent to the whole theme, embracing consciously or unconsciously the famous prayer of Ignatius of Loyola, which says that we work "not looking for any reward, save that of knowing that we do your will". His prayer leaves us thinking that we are not meant to be conscious of reward and that somehow we have found a higher ethic. But the Bible closes with a glorified Saviour returning eager to share his rewards with those who have served him acceptably. Which of us is going to tell the Lord of Glory that being preoccupied with rewards is not very nice and that we have now moved on to a higher ethical code? I for one am not rushing in to volunteer! If Jesus is for rewards and we are against them, guess who's wrong. Guess who has to change their thinking!

Modern attitudes have emerged that undermine the individual's significance and personal responsibility. For example, it is possible at the conclusion of a service to express appreciation to the keyboard player, only to hear the reply, "Oh, it wasn't me. It was the Lord." I feel like asking, "Who played the occasional wrong note?" Or even commenting, "It wasn't *that* good." In trying to avoid pride, people are tempted to embrace anonymity.

I have frequently heard preachers prayed for, prior to a service, by a group of well-meaning deacons, "Lord, this morning hide the preacher. We want to see Jesus only." A preacher friend of mine commented, "Next time that happens to me I am going to open with prayer and then duck down under the pulpit and see how well they do without me!" A more recent and growingly popular phrase claims that "God is seeking a faceless army", hinting again that God puts high value on anonymity. The reality is that God loves every face and every individual that he has called. We are not anonymous or unaccountable. It is because God loves every individual that our Bibles are littered with pages filled with almost unpronounceable names! Surely, God would spare us the embarrassment of fighting with the pronunciation of these endless lists if all he wants is "a faceless army". Each individual matters to him and each one is thoroughly accountable to him. You are not called to anonymity but to significant accountability!

It is, therefore, of huge importance that you take seriously your call to serve the living God, knowing that you will ultimately give a thorough and detailed account to him of all that you have done.

Make sure, therefore, that your labours are labours of love and your works are works of faith. If your motives are less than pure, they will be burned up and you will suffer loss, though you will be saved, as Paul is quick to add (1 Corinthians 3:15). Your salvation has nothing to do with your works, since it is always by grace through faith. You may feel like "one escaping through the flames", as the New International Version has it, but you will be saved.

Straw or gold?

Imagine that a lady from your local church or small group is currently in hospital. It occurs to you that she will soon be coming out and you have yet to visit her. Suddenly you think to yourself, "I haven't visited Mary yet. I ought to go and see her." At this point, it is important to stand back and speak to God about it. May I suggest that you always pause when you hear yourself thinking, *I ought to* do something? It may be that if you were to submit the whole thing to God he would tell you that your life is already too busy. There may be many unfinished tasks, say, in connection with your husband or your children or other matters to which you are already committed. God might tell you that there is no necessity for you to visit her, at which point you must rest and not trouble yourself, secure in the knowledge that your relationship with God is not determined by your work rate!

However, you may find a rather different response from the Lord. He might bring to the surface the fact that in reality Mary's needs were not preoccupying you. You worry what she would think about you if you did not visit her whilst she was in hospital. Soon she will be out and you will have to see her. Will her appraisal of you go down? Jesus might bring to your attention that you did not actually care about Mary at all. You had not even thought of her fears and anxieties but were really thinking about your own reputation. God might say to you that in fact he has great compassion for Mary. She is anxious and fearful about her impending operation. She needs love to be expressed to her. Jesus is looking for a channel to communicate his kindness to her and to bring his love into that hospital ward.

If so, repent and ask for God's forgiveness. Pray for Mary and ask that you might bring her something of the Lord's compassion and that his presence would accompany you as you visit her. Is the love of God going to enter that ward, or a conscience-driven Christian merely doing her duty? In reality Mary will probably know the difference! You also will know the barrenness of an unfruitful activity. Meanwhile, the angels look on in boredom, knowing that ultimately this will not survive the fire test. The secret motives of your heart will be revealed, you will suffer loss, and no reward will follow.

When we genuinely serve the living God, the will of God is fulfilled. God said of David, "I have found David, the son of Jesse, a man after my own heart, who will do all my will" (Acts 13:22). At the conclusion of his life, David earned the testimony that he "served the purpose of God in his own generation" (Acts 13:36). He had no appetite for dead works or dull routine. He was eager to do God's will. God's purposes were accomplished through him. Jesus, towards the conclusion of his ministry claimed, "I have glorified you on the earth, having accomplished the work which you have given me to do" (John 17:4). We glorify God on the earth by doing the works that he has given us to do, nothing more, nothing less. This calls for a relationship with God.

Jesus said what the Father told him and only did what the Father showed him.

Indeed, if you were to ask Jesus his secret, he would say, "I have food to eat that you do not know about", adding, "My food is to do the will of him who sent me and to accomplish his work" (John 4:32, 34). Jesus was completely nourished and fulfilled by devoting himself to the Father's will. He was sustained by being thoroughly preoccupied with accomplishing his God-given task. Aim at developing a lifestyle of trying to please the Lord and discerning what he would have you to do, so that with faith, joy and love you might do the "good works which God prepared beforehand so that we might walk in them" (Ephesians 2:10).

Towards the end of his life King Saul testified, "I have played the fool" (1 Samuel 26:21). The apostle Paul (formerly Saul) concluded his life with a contrasting testimony, namely, "I have fought the good fight, I have finished the course, I have kept the faith; in the future there is laid up for me the crown of righteousness, which the Lord, the righteous judge, will award to me on that day" (2 Timothy 4:7, 8). What a contrast! One man called Saul ending his life in despair, another man called Saul ending his life joyfully, anticipating the reward of the crown which the Lord Jesus will give him.

Let me urge you as you enjoy the grace of God not to miss out on his best for you but to celebrate a clear conscience and serve the Lord with gladness, looking for the reward.

7

What have I done to deserve this?

God's grace often amazes us. In the mystery of his love he has chosen the foolish, the weak, the despised, and even those who "are not"! He wants you to put no confidence in your own resources but to glory in his prior wisdom and pleasure to demonstrate grace to those he chooses to bless.

In this chapter we shall be reminded of God's unusual and unexpected ways of blessing not the "beautiful people" but the unlovely and the unwanted.

What have I done to deserve this?

Maybe you remember the smash hit musical *The Sound of Music* in which, in a moment of joyful gratitude, Julie Andrew reflects, "I must have done something good." She can't imagine why things have turned out so well for her. Perhaps in her youth or childhood lies the secret of her being worthy.

It's not rare for people to think that way. An inner sense of the need for fair play seems to demand that you get what you deserve. Grace stands in stark contrast and says, "I will not only release you completely from what you deserve but also give you in its place overwhelming mercy, kindness, covenant loyalty, favour and everlasting blessings beyond your wildest dreams." Grace is simply and beautifully expressed in Judy Pruett's song:

> The grace of God upon my life
> Is not dependent upon me,
> On what I have done or deserved,
> But a gift of mercy from God
> Which has been given unto me
> Because of his love, his love for me.
>
> It is unending, unfailing, unlimited, unmerited,

The grace of God given unto me.
(Copyright © 1990 Judy Pruett/
Kingsway's Thankyou Music)

God's grace defies our understanding. Why does he favour us? Why does he commit himself to everlasting love? The explanation offered to the Israelites was more of a riddle than an explanation: "The Lord did not set his love on you nor choose you because you were more in number than any of the peoples, for you were the fewest of all peoples, but because the Lord loved you and kept the oath which the Lord swore to your forefathers . . ." (Deuteronomy 7:7–8). So the Lord set his love on you because he loved you! Or as Eugene Peterson has it, "He did it out of sheer love" (Eugene H Peterson, *The Message: The Bible in Contemporary Language*, NavPress, 2002). God chose Israel to be "a people for his own possession out of all the peoples who are on the face of the earth" (Deuteronomy 7:6). They were his "special treasure" (margin). He delighted in them and treasured them, as he does all his chosen children. He gave his heart to them in covenant love. He prized them and watched over them jealously. They were his particular pride and joy. It is hard for us to comprehend the intensity of God's love for those he commits himself to. One of God's mysteries, not so much to be analysed as to be enjoyed and celebrated, is that the Lord loves you because he loves you!

Abraham's life was turned upside down and he became the father of all who believe, not because he was the most impressive man around but because God chose to favour him. Not that God's favour meant that his life would be a bed of roses. Abraham's life was hardly an easy ride. From beginning to end he was tested and tried, but was wonderfully favoured and called God's friend.

In a later generation God's grace and favour fell particularly upon Jacob rather than his twin brother Esau, not because he deserved it, as Paul was quick to underline, but "before the twins were born or had done anything good or bad . . ." (Romans 9:11, NIV). Once again, as you compare Esau's life with Jacob's, you might wonder who was being favoured. Esau's life was one of untroubled prosperity while Jacob's was characterised by constant trials. He had to flee his home and was cheated by his uncle regarding his wages and even the choice of his bride. Later in life he lost his beloved son Joseph and appeared even to lose Benjamin. Heartbreak seemed to follow heartbreak. But throughout his life he developed an insatiable appetite for fellowship with God and was blessed with a changed name. Jacob, the cheat, became Israel, the Prince with God. He experienced amazing supernatural encounters and received awesome promises. In spite of being poured from vessel to vessel, he was clearly the favoured one. As an old man, leaning on his staff, he was approached by mighty Pharaoh, who urged him to bless him. His spiritual dignity and standing were evident to Egypt's king, and the Creator of the universe embraced the title, "the God of Israel".

In the next generation God's particular favour fell upon Joseph. He was the one chosen by God to receive special grace. Once again we notice that this blessing by no means guaranteed a trouble-free path, rather the opposite. His life was apparently shaped by other people's envy, jealousy, ruthlessness, hurt pride, unrequited lust, anger and injustice. Tossed about like so much flotsam on a fast-flowing river, he found himself dumped and forgotten far from home in the depths of a foreign prison.

Amazingly, he was still the object of God's wonderful grace and was sustained through the trials until he arrived at God's appointed place of fulfilment as ruler over Egypt and saviour of Israel. Called by grace, he was also sustained by grace to the end.

God's choice

Maybe the story of David's call demonstrates God's grace more wonderfully than any other Old Testament figure. Samuel, the most significant man of God in his generation, came to Jesse's home to meet with his sons and select Saul's replacement as Israel's next king, but David was not even invited to the party.

David's call serves to underline the unexpectedness of God's choice and how the most unlikely can be objects of his grace.

> For consider your calling, brethren, that there were not many wise according to the flesh, not many mighty, not many noble; but God has chosen the foolish things of the world to shame the wise, and God has chosen the weak things of the world to shame the things which were strong, and the base things of the world and the despised God has chosen, the things that are not, so that he may nullify the things that are so that no man can boast before God. (1 Corinthians 1:26–29)

God's choices surprise us. His grace defies our logical analysis or even guesswork. "God has chosen the foolish things of the world to shame the wise." Our interview boards are not looking for the foolish. Industry's headhunters are not searching for them. They are impressed by the wise, but Paul says, "Not many of you were wise by human standards" (1 Corinthians 1:26, NIV).

If God chooses the foolish, we don't have to write ourselves off so quickly. Many Christians deplore their lack of brainpower. Because they are not very smart, they regard themselves as disqualified. Paul says just the opposite. He tells us that the wisdom of the world is foolishness to God who has declared war on it. "I will destroy the wisdom of the wise and the cleverness of the clever I will set aside" (1 Corinthians 1:19). The clever are inclined to dismiss the gospel as foolishness. They find it hard to submit their intellectual perspectives to the authority of God's word, and regard a cross-centred message utterly irrelevant, whereas those who humble themselves and embrace the gospel discover that the cross is the wisdom of God.

Grace cuts through the normal categories and teaches us that those who are naturally bright do not have a head start in the Christian life. The foolish are preferred. What should be our response? If you are one of the few naturally bright people who were chosen, be deeply grateful and make sure not to lean on your own intellect. Submit your perspectives to God. Beware the dangers of forcing your opinions on others or dismissing the apparently ignorant who have little education. Remember that God hides things from the wise and prudent and reveals them to babes (Matthew 11:25). So make sure you approach God like a little child who acknowledges its need for help.

If, on the contrary, you are one who has always despised your own insights and intellectual skills, celebrate this wonderful upside-down kingdom. You don't have so much to unlearn. Perhaps you don't have so many strong opinions that need to be jettisoned. Come in simple faith to Jesus. Let him be your teacher, let the Holy Spirit be your guide, learn truth from God that is not measured by intellectual skill but is rooted in attitude and obedience. "The fear of the Lord is the beginning of knowledge" (Proverbs 1:7). As Derek Kidner, commenting on that verse, says in a sentence packed with insight, "Knowledge in its fullness is a relationship dependent on revelation and inseparable from character." The Book of Proverbs tells us that "Wisdom calls aloud in the street" (Proverbs 1:20). God wants us to be "streetwise". As Derek Kidner says again, "Wisdom is for the business of living, not for an elite for the pursuit of scholarship" (Derek Kidner, *Proverbs*, IVP, 1972).

"God has chosen the weak things of the world to shame the things that are strong" (1 Corinthians 1:27). How many Christians deplore their apparent weakness? How they wish they were more resourceful and stronger! Fearfully conscious of personal inadequacy, they regard themselves as disqualified for the kingdom of God.

As Christians, we often betray how impressed we are by the apparently strong when we long for prominent people to be saved. We anticipate the amazing influence that a famous pop star, sports idol or fascinating media personality could have if he or she became a Christian. Sadly, Christian leaders have often been hasty in giving visibility to a recently converted celebrity, forgetting that they may be significant in the world's eyes but they have yet to be rooted in God. Quickly transferring their high profile to the Christian circuit, they often come unstuck. God is not impressed with human magnetism in the same way that we are and does not necessarily feel obliged to endorse it.

No confidence in the flesh

Often God's programme for the strong is first to weaken them so that he can use them. Moses is a case in point. We meet him as a young man instructed in all the wisdom of Egypt and described as mighty in word and deed. A forceful born leader, his first endeavour to help the Hebrews ends in total disaster and he flees to the wilderness. After forty years of futility God calls him and invites him to be his representative in the greatest demonstration of divine power the world had ever seen. But what is Moses' response? He doesn't want the job. He asks to be excused. He claims that he can't speak. All his natural strength has gone. This formerly mighty man is now weak enough to be God's instrument in confronting Pharaoh, weak enough to know that the Red Sea is God's problem, not his. Strong people can accomplish much, but eventually they reach the end of their personal resourcefulness. Sometimes it is a huge shock to them to discover suddenly that they do not have what it takes. Weak people have to trust in God. They know from the start that they haven't got it but God's grace must see them through.

So, if God chooses the weak, don't deplore your weakness. Instead, celebrate God's grace in choosing you and believe he will supply grace for the future, knowing that his strength is perfected in your weakness. Believe it! Weakness is a great advantage! It helps you build your life on the right foundation from the beginning.

Peter, confident in his own strength, boasted that he would never fail Jesus even if the others did. His crumbling failure is recorded for all to read, so also is the renewed call of a gracious Saviour who picks up his now weakened follower and freshly commissions him. He is now weak enough in his own eyes to be God's spokesman on the day of Pentecost.

As we proceed through Paul's list, we find "not many are of noble birth"; instead, God prefers the lowly and the outsiders. Some people place a lot of importance on family background and associations. They like to be in with the right people or to have friends in high places, but not many noble people are chosen. God chooses the base, those whom nobody else wants to befriend. The Jews would spit at a tax collector but Jesus would seek and find him.

Maybe you are ashamed of your background and feel you were born on the wrong side of the track. Maybe you strive to climb the ladder, learn the art of name-dropping, and hide your past. Beware the serious danger of trying to find your ultimate security and identity in anything other than the wonder that Jesus loves you and has chosen you for himself.

Paul's list goes even deeper down the spiral of hopelessness in telling us that "God chose the despised things". Some of us are despised in our own eyes, let alone in the eyes of anyone else. We have given up hope. Maybe you feel you have been used and dumped, not valued for yourself at all but treated like a commodity, now past your sell-by date. One commentary describes the word "despised" as "expressly branded with contempt". The same word is used in Luke 23:11: "The soldiers treated him with contempt and mocked him." They looked on Jesus as a stupid fool, and despised and crucified him.

As D A Carson says,

> Where proud men and women parade their mighty intellects, God chooses the simple; where wealthy people assess each other on the basis of their respective holdings, God chooses the poor; where self-centred leaders lust for power, God chooses the nobodies. . . . Salvation is God's free gift, secured by the ignominious death of his own Son. This odious death is God's triumphant act, his most dazzling and powerful deed, the action by which he disgraces and trashes all human pretension. God's salvation springs from God's grace and it is received by those who trust him – not by the "beautiful people" or the rich and powerful. (D A Carson, *The Cross and Christian Ministry*, Baker, 1993)

Things that are not

Finally, we reach the end of Paul's list: "He chose the things that are not" – people who are totally overlooked and who don't figure in anyone's thinking. You can't get any lower than "not"! Maybe that's exactly how you feel. You arrive at church and everybody else seems to have their friend or group of associates. You feel isolated and afraid in entering the group. Maybe you think, "Nobody really wants to talk to me. It's so embarrassing just standing here." When you find yourself in such a mood you are so vulnerable to Satan who will add to your predicament by telling you that you are not worth thinking about and beyond hope. Why do you bother even to come to church? No one even notices whether you are here or not.

David's breathtaking discovery was that, though his father ignored him, God had greater plans. Picture Samuel, the great national leader, inviting Jesse and his sons to a sacrifice. What a privilege! If I thought that the queen was going to visit my house I would want all of my family there, but David was left as though he did not exist.

Maybe your father was always indifferent to you. Maybe you have carried rejection for a long time and feel that nobody really cares.

Perhaps Jesse, as he paraded his seven sons, regarded seven as the perfect number. David was number eight. He was left out, unwanted, looking after a few sheep. Maybe you have been made to feel unwanted. I have had to bring pastoral care to some who have been told by their parents not only that they were unwanted, but that their unplanned arrival had ruined their lives. Some have experienced hatred and rejection from such an early age that they feel that they are of no consequence and have nothing to offer.

As Samuel went down the line from one son to another, he knew that none of them was God's choice. Perplexed, he asked if there was another and, to everyone's surprise, he chose the one who "was not". The one whom Samuel would not even have known existed was God's choice. God has chosen the things that are not.

Years later, David longed to build a house for God. The prophet Nathan encouraged him to go for it, but quickly received divine correction. Instead, God informs David of his own plans and purposes:

> I took you from the pasture and from following the flock to be ruler over my people Israel. I have been with you wherever you have gone, and I have cut off all your enemies from before you. Now I will make your name great, like the names of the greatest men of the earth. And I will provide a place for my people Israel and will plant them so that they can have a home of their own and no longer be disturbed. Wicked people shall not oppress them any more, as they did at the beginning and have done ever since the time I appointed leaders over my people Israel. I will also give you rest from all your enemies . . . the Lord himself will establish a house for you: When your days

are over and you rest with your fathers, I will raise up your offspring to succeed you, who will come from your own body, and I will establish his kingdom. He is the one who will build a house for my Name, and I will establish the throne of his kingdom for ever. I will be his father, and he shall be my son. When he does wrong, I will punish him with the rod of men . . . But my love will never be taken away from him, as I took it away from Saul, whom I removed from before you. Your house and your kingdom shall endure for ever before me; your throne shall be established for ever. (2 Samuel 7:8–16)

David sat in wonder, overwhelmed at the grace that had pursued him all the days of his life. God had taken his breath away and all he could ask was, "Is this your usual way of dealing with man?" (2 Samuel 7:19).

You may wonder what you have done to deserve God's love. How is it that God has shown you such kindness? This is the very stuff of grace, that he amazes you, contradicts every expectation, seeks you out, finds you and lavishes his love upon you. You have done nothing and can do nothing to earn his grace. The secret of his grace to you lies deep in the mystery of his foreknowledge. Simply receive it, celebrate it, delight yourself in it and live as one whom God is pleased to favour from his own overflowing resources of kindness.

8

By the grace of God I am what I am

Grace does not simply provide forgiveness; it gives you a new identity altogether. It also calls you to a sphere of service and giftedness. Our responsibility is to make sure that this freely-given grace is not squandered.

In this chapter we not only celebrate the wonderful gift of a new identity in Christ, but also point out some of the pitfalls to be avoided so that you do not dissipate his gifts. Paul makes it clear that God's grace will supply your need right to the end.

By the grace of God I am what I am

When Moses encountered God at the burning bush, he asked, "Who shall I say is sending me?" God, underived, uncreated, unaffected, uncontaminated and unthreatened, answered, "I am that I am." One of the biggest philosophical questions people ask themselves is, "Who am I?" Many search for an answer before they come to Christ and some are still asking the same question when they have become Christians. It's a vital one. Paul's response is the extraordinary claim, "By the grace of God I am what I am" (1 Corinthians 15:10). Grace gives him peace and security regarding his identity.

Earlier in his life, Paul would have regarded himself very differently. In Philippians 3, for instance, he describes what he used to be, "circumcised the eighth day, of the nation of Israel, of the tribe of Benjamin, a Hebrew of the Hebrews, and as regards the righteousness which is in the law, found blameless" (Philippians 3:5, 6). He wasn't a man searching for answers; he knew his identity. He knew his background. He was trained at the feet of Gamaliel, probably the foremost Jewish teacher of his generation, and he could boast that he was ahead of his contemporaries.

But Paul also had dreadful sin in his life. He had persecuted the church. When Stephen, a magnificent young man full of the Holy Spirit, wisdom and power, was stoned to death, Paul was overseeing the event. Surely, Paul was trying to suppress unremitting guilt when God said to him at his conversion, "It is hard for you to kick against the goads" (Acts 26:14). Paul's vulnerability may have been rooted in his memory of that day. Stephen died with breathtaking dignity, his face shining like an angel. Perhaps that image was stamped indelibly on his conscience.

Grace and identity

How powerful grace is that it can take an embittered legalist, a murderer, and set him free to say, "By the grace of God I am what I am"! Grace not only provided forgiveness, grace gave him a new identity. He was a new person, a new creation. Sometimes people think, "I could never forgive myself for that", "I ruined that young girl's life", "I broke my parents' hearts", "I cheated that guy in business". Some people feel shackled to guilty memories.

If that is your experience, you must not only receive forgiveness for the past but also the new identity that God freely gives you. No other evaluation of your life can compete with his, namely, "Therefore if any one is in Christ he is a new creature, old things have passed away, behold new things have come" (2 Corinthians 5:17). Do not withstand this wonderful grace! God's assessment of you is the authentic one. Because Paul believed it, he was able to leave behind the past.

God told Abram, whose name means "exalted father", "You will be 'Abraham'", which means "father of a multitude". Abraham believed God, and by faith he received his new identity. God renamed Jacob "Israel". He took a cheat like Jacob and called him "Prince with God". When God gives you a new identity, receive it! God called Gideon "a mighty man of valour" even while he was skulking in a cave. God's assessment overcame his previous view of himself. When God says you are mighty, believe it! "By the grace of God I am what I am."

Grace and ministry

But in this passage Paul not only addresses the issue of his identity in Christ, he also refers to his ministry as an apostle. Grace not only saved him, it also called him to a sphere of service. He says in Romans 1:5 that he "received grace and apostleship". Or again, 1 Corinthians 3:10, "Grace was given to me to be a wise master builder." Again, Ephesians 3:8, "Grace was given me: to preach . . . the unsearchable riches of Christ." He saw the whole operation as a grace gift.

We are not all apostles, but we have gifts that differ according to the grace that has been given to us (Romans 12:6). 1 Peter 4:10 says, "As each one of us has received a special gift, employ it in serving one another as good stewards of the manifold [or multicoloured] grace of God." Gifts of grace have been distributed by God to his church. Each of us has the responsibility of stewardship of the gifts we have received. We have the joyful privilege of using those gifts for the good of the body of Christ.

God's gifts are not rewards. They are not proofs of holiness or marks of maturity, only given to the most advanced Christians to demonstrate God's approval of their spiritual progress. If gifts were distributed on that basis, the Corinthian church would have been completely devoid of charismata (gifts of the Spirit), but Paul said that they lacked none of the gifts, in spite of their immaturity and, indeed, carnality. As D A Carson says, they were "wretchedly, unacceptably, spiritually immature" (D A Carson, *The Cross and Christian Ministry*, Baker, 1993). Gifts are *freely* given on the basis of grace. If you are in Christ, his righteousness not only saves you, it also qualifies you to receive amazing gifts of the Holy Spirit.

"His grace to me was not in vain"

Having received grace, Paul was eager to make sure that God's grace to him was not in vain. How is it possible to make God's grace in vain? A variety of responses can frustrate the work of God's grace in our lives. One way is when we don't receive it, simply because we don't believe it. When God called Moses, his response was that he couldn't possibly complete the task on offer. He could not speak to Pharaoh. If you don't believe God can use you, you will frustrate the grace of God. Gideon initially complained that he was the least in his father's house and that God couldn't use him. He was in danger of grace coming to him in vain. Beware the danger of missing it by questioning, "Who am I to do this?"

Paul speaks of the danger of the foot feeling disqualified because it's not a hand and therefore not part of the body, or the ear regretting that it is not an eye (see 1 Corinthians 12:16). Beware the danger of thinking that because you are not as prominent as the next person, God's grace is not functioning through you.

Don't turn amazing grace into cheap grace

A second snare to avoid is carelessness or licence. I can make grace in vain by having a casual attitude. Paul warned the Galatians, "You were called to freedom, brethren, only do not turn your freedom into an opportunity for the flesh, but through love serve one another" (Galatians 5:13). Peter says, "Act as free men but don't use your freedom as a covering for evil" (1 Peter 2:16). Jude verse 4 speaks of "ungodly persons who turn the grace of God into licentiousness". Don't turn amazing grace into cheap grace. Don't develop the attitude that it doesn't really matter; God will always forgive me; grace covers it; I can do whatever I like. This makes grace in vain. Paul says this: "All things are lawful but not all things are profitable. All things are lawful but

I will not be mastered by anything" (1 Corinthians 6:12).
Paul celebrates his new-found freedom from the restrictions
of law, but refuses to drift into bondage to sin.

Don't fall into legalism

A third thing that can make God's grace in vain is legalism.
The Galatians had been born again and had experienced
a lavish outflow of the Holy Spirit through the ministry of
the apostle Paul. He was appalled, therefore, when he discovered that they were reverting to the law. Some formerly
Jewish Christians had come into the church in Galatia and
thoroughly confused and intimidated the formerly pagan
Christians by teaching that if they were to be fully acceptable to God, they must observe circumcision, the Sabbath,
and the special eating rules. Paul was outraged. He insist-
ed, "I do not nullify the grace of God, for if righteousness
comes through the law, Christ died needlessly" (Galatians
2:21). By embracing law in an effort to make themselves
worthy of God, they were making his grace in vain. "You
who are seeking to be justified by law have fallen away from
grace," he thundered (Galatians 5:4). The phrase "falling
from grace" had a very different meaning for Paul than its
popular use.

Beware false doctrine

The fourth danger is that of drifting into theological error.
Paul claimed that he went to Jerusalem and submitted what
he was teaching to those who were apostles before him, in
case he was running in vain (see Galatians 2:2). Although
he was personally commissioned by Christ, he recognised
the necessity of checking with Peter, James and John, who
were "in Christ" before him, to make sure that he wasn't
running in vain or, though he was zealous, that he was not
getting off course. You can be enthusiastic but wrong!

Paul described the Jews of his generation as "having a
zeal for God but not according to knowledge". So all their

energy was a waste of time. People can give all their devotion to something that will ultimately prove to be in vain because it's not what God requires. You can develop fierce commitment to false doctrine or dead religion, so watch out! It is tragic to see a new believer who starts well begin to be devoured by a particular doctrinal emphasis and spend his or her whole life as a single-issue Christian.

Hard work is no enemy of grace

Lastly, Paul said, "His grace to me was not in vain because I worked harder than any of them." Hard work is no enemy of grace! Laziness is a way of making grace in vain. Paul was unashamed to speak of his hard work. He did not regard it as being in competition with grace but enumerated his toils, struggles, labours, shipwrecks, beatings and journeys. If you are thoroughly rooted in grace, you needn't be afraid of hard work. He was strong in grace but also burning with zeal.

Yet not I

Having boasted of his hard work, Paul suddenly adds, "yet not I". This is where it gets puzzling. Paul, is it you who's working hard or somebody else? "Well, I worked hard, but it's not I, but the grace of God that's with me."

How are we to understand this? Perhaps we should start by explaining what we are *not* saying. We are not saying, "I received grace", as if grace was something that happened only in the past, suggesting, "Thank you, Lord, I was a sinner, I was a legalist, I was a killer of Christians, but I obtained grace! Thank you, Lord, what mercy! Now, to show appreciation for all that grace from yesterday, I am now going to work harder than any of them." That's *not* what he is saying. Paul's hard work was not just outworking his indebtedness to God. He was not working hard simply to show his appreciation for grace.

The grace that saved me and gave me a gift of ministry is the same grace that will now come *with* me into my future. We live by grace all the time! We serve by grace all the time. Nor is Paul saying that, having laboured and toiled, you come up for air gasping for some grace and then sink down to work again, only to come up again for a bit more grace! No. We live with grace. Grace works *with* me. Grace is my partner. Sometimes you feel you are hardly working at all because God's grace is working with you.

How does grace work with me? Through attitude and action. Jerry Bridges says, "Your worst days are never so bad that you are beyond the reach of God's grace, and your best days are never so good that you are beyond the need of God's grace" (Jerry Bridges, *The Discipline of Grace*, NavPress, 1994). Staying humble, we must acknowledge our need of grace all the time. We don't say, "Thank you, Lord, grace brought me this far. Now it's over to me." Paul claimed to have learned to be content in whatever circumstances he was. He knew how to get along with humble means and how to get along with plenty. He claimed to have learned this secret (see Philippians 4:11). He goes on, "I can do all things through him who strengthens me." We often quote that verse when contemplating the aggressive advance of the kingdom, claiming, "I can do all things through Christ." The actual context of Paul's words in Philippians was that he had learned to be content. He had learned how to pace himself. He could do all things in terms of sustaining his ministry in the midst of difficulties. It was not about dramatic power ministry. It was about the challenge of day-to-day routine. Have you learned to be content? Can you cope? For example, how do you get three children to school when you are tired, how do you feed and clothe them with little money, how do you cope with an ill parent, with increasing pressure at work, with abusive neighbours? How do you cope?

Don't lose heart

Sometimes we are tested and are tempted to throw in the towel in terms of receiving grace. Paul gives us a little insight into some of the conflicts he went through when he tells us that sometimes it was like being squeezed so much that he cried, "Who is adequate for these things?" (2 Corinthians 2:16). But he gets an answer: "Our adequacy is from God who also made us adequate" (2 Corinthians 3:5–6).

In 2 Corinthians 4:16, Paul claims, "Therefore we do not lose heart", adding, "Though our outer man is decaying, our inner man is being renewed day by day." That's how grace works. Sometimes he was tested in the extreme: "We were burdened excessively beyond our strength so that we despaired even of life; indeed, we had the sentence of death within ourselves so that we would not trust in ourselves, but in God who raises the dead" (2 Corinthians 1:8–9). Sometimes that describes how you feel! This does not apply only to apostles; this is for believers trying to run a business, raise children, work with difficult colleagues, keep a godly attitude when wrongly accused, or when the car has been broken into . . . again! When you keep thinking you have got nothing left to give, grace is like those wonderful birthday cake candles, which you blow out, only to discover that they all come on again! It's not I, but the grace of God that's with me, even in pressure.

At times, the pressure was so intense for Paul that, in 2 Corinthians 12:9, he asked for the thorn in his flesh to be removed, but the verse continues unexpectedly, "He has said to me, 'My grace is sufficient for you, for power is perfected in weakness.' Most gladly therefore I will rather boast about my weaknesses so that the power of Christ may dwell in me." We don't know what Paul's thorn in the flesh was; but when he said, "I prayed three times", we are talking about some serious prayer on three occasions. The phrase I have underlined in my Bible is, "He has said to me". We need not only to know in theory that God's grace is sufficient; we must also experience the intimacy of his presence and the expression of his love that communicates the grace. When we hear his voice and receive his renewing touch, everything else falls into the right proportion. Truly, his grace is sufficient.

Writing from prison to the Philippian church, Paul seems to be constantly overflowing with joy. It is difficult to imagine how gruelling his circumstances must have been, as his imprisonment kept him hovering between life and death. Maybe he would die, but of one thing he was confident: "If I am to live on in the flesh, this will mean fruitful labour for me" (Philippians 1:22). He knew he might die, but if he lived he expected to be fruitful. Why was he so confident? Because he had received grace and apostleship to bring about the obedience of faith among the Gentiles (see Romans 1:5). Gentiles would become obedient to the faith. Paul was confident that if he lived it would happen. This was what he had received grace to accomplish.

Paul expected to be fruitful and to see lives transformed through his ministry. That was why he was on the planet. God had given him grace to be fruitful and Paul was sure that that grace was not going to be in vain. Like Nehemiah, he could confidently say, "The God of heaven will give us success. Therefore we, his servants, will arise and build" (Nehemiah 2:20).

By the grace of God you are what you are. Mighty grace has given you a new identity. Don't let that grace be in vain in your life.

9

Grace and the prevailing culture

Christians are supposed to be "in the world but not of it". What does this really mean? What does grace teach us regarding the problem of "worldliness"?

In this chapter we see the futility of a religion of mere rule keeping and the vital role of a healthy conscience. We shall also see that the cross of Christ sets us free from the snares of a world that has no future.

Grace and the prevailing culture

"Worldly" was a new word to me when I was first converted, but one that, it seems, I had to learn. As a Christian I was not to be "worldly", but I had to learn what was and what wasn't "worldly". It wasn't always obvious and as the years have gone by, I have realised that definitions change from nation to nation and tradition to tradition, and also get adjusted as fashions change. What is often referred to as worldliness could more accurately be understood as the specific "no go" areas as defined by your particular church culture.

When once preaching in an Eastern European setting I had to learn that to wear a tie in church was to be drawing attention to yourself and displaying a somewhat arrogant attitude. I noticed that all the men in the congregation were wearing jackets but none wore ties. Ties were narcissistic, unacceptable and definitely worldly.

On another occasion, whilst speaking at a conference in Bloemfontein, South Africa, I had addressed several week-day seminars where those attending were wearing shorts and short-sleeved shirts. The pastor who hosted the conference wore casual trousers and an open-necked, short-sleeved shirt. On the Sunday morning at breakfast in his home he sat in a vest and shorts. Soon it was time for the meeting.

I dressed "smart casual" as I had throughout the week and ran to catch him, now waiting in his car. His look of alarm as he greeted me was unmistakable as he sat at the wheel of his car in the colossal heat in a three-piece suit and tie. I paused and asked if my dress was acceptable.

"I have never addressed my people without wearing a tie," was his somewhat stern reply. I rushed back and changed, adding the required jacket and tie.

Appropriate clothing certainly seemed significant when I was first converted. To be tie-less on Sunday would have been frowned upon and jeans were certainly not acceptable.

Not only did inappropriate clothing represent worldliness, certain "unholy" objects were clearly regarded as worldly. I still remember the first time I saw a young man bringing a guitar to church. As he approached the steps to the main entrance, the wife of the church's leading deacon stood on the top step.

"You are not bringing *that* in *here*!" she thundered. The young man was cowed and withdrew in shame.

Guitars were clearly worldly and the church building was regarded as God's house, a place where whispering and reverent tiptoeing were regarded as appropriate. The squeaking shoe of a deacon "distributing the elements" at communion would certainly have been noticed. A nod or half smile to a friend was allowed, but speech was outlawed. Having received one's hymnbook at the door, one expressed appreciation with a whispered "Thank you", proceeded to one's seat and bowed in prayer for a length of time deemed reverent, and then waited for the service to begin and run its course.

This was a Baptist church, unlike Anglicans whom we regarded as very formal with their bowing to the altar!

At a similar time, early in my Christian experience, I had stopped on my way to church to buy some petrol for my motorbike. A lady from the church who happened to be passing asked what I was doing.

"Getting petrol," was my naïve reply.

"Don't you know it's the Sabbath?" she sniffed.

I hadn't a clue what she was talking about, but soon learned that there was a rather arbitrary list of things forbidden on Sundays and regarded as thoroughly inappropriate for Christians.

I have read that, having invited Billy Graham to conduct his first great crusade in the UK in the 1950s, some leading British Christians discovered that Billy Graham's wife, Ruth, actually wore make-up, even lipstick! She also had a modern haircut! During her sea journey to the UK panic ensued. What could be done? It would appear that at the time, British Christians would have been scandalised by such worldliness.

Denominations have split and new groups have formed over the issue of whether ladies may or may not wear earrings.

When I was first saved, going to the cinema was definitely worldly. Classical music was OK but jazz was beyond the pale. In some churches I have been expected to call men and women not simply by their Christian names but as "Brother or Sister Such-and-such". When once preaching in Mobile, Alabama, I publicly asked to be forgiven if I omitted to precede people's names by the required "Brother" or "Sister" since I had never learned to do it and would probably forget. I had grown up with a brother and a sister but it had never occurred to me to call them anything other than their actual name. Once, while talking with an Indian Christian lady in Bombay, she at one point simply called me "Terry", only to pause very embarrassed and correct herself, "Sorry, Brother Terry".

Religious minefield

Does grace have anything to say to this religious minefield? Who makes up the rules? Do they matter? How many do you have to learn? Or can you forget them all and say, "A plague on all legalists!'"?

Paul addresses the theme in Romans. Indeed, some would argue that one of the main purposes of the epistle was to handle such problems and appeal for mutual acceptance and unity. Aware that the church in Rome consisted of a mixture of former Jews and former Gentiles, he realised there would be huge tensions. Former Gentiles with their carefree and law-free background would have to mix in close proximity with former Jews whose previous devotion to God was expressed through detailed law-keeping. They would undoubtedly be proceeding with a tender conscience towards such things as eating formerly forbidden meats and having new liberal attitudes to Sabbath-keeping. The issue of eating meat that had possibly been previously offered to idols was a particularly hot potato!

What was Paul's approach?

First, he acknowledged the fact that some were stronger in faith than others. The strong in faith were clear that they could, for instance, eat all things, while the weak would only eat vegetables (Romans 14:1–2). Some regarded one day above another while others regarded all days alike (Romans 14:5). Paul's great preoccupation was that they should not judge one another but pursue things that made for peace and mutual upbuilding. The strong should bear with the weak and not simply please themselves (Romans 15:1).

Obeying your conscience

The conscience is clearly a very delicate mechanism in the human psyche. It is intuitive rather than rational. As a gift of God it must be obeyed. When the "red light" of conscience registers, it is essential not to override it. For instance, if your conscience suddenly awakens you that you should never have raised your voice and spoken to your friend like that, you should not try reasoning with yourself, "She started it. It's her fault." If your conscience is troubling you, obey it, don't reason with it. If your conscience tells you that you shouldn't be stealing those things from your office, don't argue with it, "Mr So-and-so does it and he's a Christian, so it must be OK." An ignored or rejected conscience can soon become a seared conscience, which is a very dangerous thing, leaving you vulnerable to complete shipwreck (see 1 Timothy 1:19).

Having said that, the conscience is not necessarily fool-proof. It needs to be subjected to Scripture and educated by the word of God. A conscience can be wrongly programmed and lead you into bondage. It may need to be reprogrammed to line up with Scripture but it must not be abused and trodden underfoot.

Let me illustrate from the issue of drinking wine, a very delicate subject in some places. Before I was saved I drank quite a lot and was often drunk. This continued into my early years as a Christian. Then, after a crisis of conviction about my whole Christian life, I made a thoroughgoing commitment to Christ, as a result of which, among other things, I gave up drinking alcohol. I became teetotal and took out a car insurance which reflected that fact. I would not even toast the bride and groom at weddings.

Some years later, through biblical conviction, I changed my view of that subject and felt free once again to drink wine, while obviously obeying the biblical teaching which plainly outlaws drunkenness. Having not drunk wine for many years, it seemed strange once again to have a glass in my hand, but my conscience was clear.

If I had simply argued, "Other Christians drink, why don't I?" I would have offended my own conscience and done myself serious harm. I had to be satisfied from the Bible that this was acceptable and re-educate my conscience from the word of God. Similarly, if I now tried to force another Christian into my liberty on the issue while he or she was not fully persuaded, I could do him or her great harm. I can certainly point to particular scriptures and provide reasons but I must not force another person's conscience into my freedom.

This principle would apply to a number of subjects and I use the drinking of alcohol simply as an example. We must be convinced in our own minds regarding what the Bible teaches and live our lives before God in the light of his truth, respecting others who disagree.

Weaker brethren and false brethren

Paul, motivated by evangelistic passion, was willing even to change his ground in order to win people. For example, he placed himself under the law at times, in order to win those who were under the law. Timothy perhaps rejoiced to hear Paul's clear teaching that circumcision was unnecessary for the Christian believer. Perhaps he rejoiced a little less when Paul decided it would be good for Timothy to be circumcised for the gospel's sake, in order to try to win the Jews!

Paul had compassion on weaker brothers who had a troubled conscience and struggled with the gospel's liberty. He went out of his way to win them. It should be noted, however, that his attitude was very different towards those who strongly contested his liberty. He distinguished between "weaker brethren" and "false brethren", as is evident in his letter to the Galatians: "But it was because of the false brethren secretly brought in, who had sneaked in to spy out our liberty which we have in Christ Jesus, in order to bring us into bondage. But we did not yield in subjection to them for even an hour, so that the truth of the gospel would

---

1 The weaker brother, or the Christian with a weak conscience, is often misunderstood by modern Christians to be referring to the more vulnerable (perhaps younger) Christian who might be easily tempted to sin. The contexts of such passages as Romans 14 and 1 Corinthians 8 make it very clear that in Paul's mind the weaker brother with the shaky conscience is the one who tends to legalism and has not been fully released by a revelation of God's grace in the New Covenant. Simply to read slowly through Romans 14 and 1 Corinthians 8 will make this clear.

remain with you" (Galatians 2: 4–5).[1] The whole letter to
the Galatians is a heart cry to these young believers to resist
every attempt to bring them back into legalism.

Paul's dismissive attitude to the legalists in Philippi is
amazing, regarding them as he does as "dogs" and "evil
workers" (Philippians 3:2). As Gordon Fee says, "This met-
aphor is full of 'bite' since dogs were zoological 'low life',
scavengers that were generally detested by Greco-Roman
society and considered unclean by Jews, who sometimes
used 'dog' to designate Gentiles." He adds, "Dogs get uni-
versally bad press in the Bible!" (Gordon D Fee, *Paul's
Letter to the Philippians*, NICNT, Eerdmans, 1995)

To Paul, the issues are very clear. Grace introduces believers into amazing freedom, breaking the bondage of legalism. This liberty has not only to be celebrated but fought
for, as the letter to the Galatians demonstrates. Having said
that, the Christian conscience is to be handled with great
sensitivity, while unity and forbearance should characterise
the church as we all prioritise to accept one another.

Worldliness, as defined by Scripture, is not preoccupied
with the imposition of lists of rules. Instead, it seems to be
focused on three main areas: worldly wealth, worldly wisdom and worldly religion.

Worldly wealth

While the New Testament certainly provides no call to a life
of asceticism, worldly riches are regarded as a dangerous
snare. Mammon is a god looking for your allegiance. You
cannot serve the true God and mammon. The rich in this
present world were evidently accepted within the churches
but were warned not to be conceited or set their hope on the
uncertainty of riches (see 1 Timothy 6:17).

Beware the danger of being duped into letting financial
issues rule your life. This is worldliness as biblically defined.
Possessions, promotions and prestige are not to dominate
your decisions. Careers, cars and mod cons must not dictate

your value system. That is to be worldly, living as though this present world has all the answers and establishes the value system.

Don't underestimate its power. Paul lost one of his close co-workers to its seduction: "Demas, because he loved this world, has deserted me . . ." (2 Timothy 4:10, NIV).

Worldly wisdom

Second, "worldly wisdom" will never allow you to boast in a faith centred in the cross. It is utter foolishness to the world. God's wisdom stands in stark contrast to the world's wisdom. "The world through its wisdom did not know him." Indeed, "Has not God made foolish the wisdom of the world?" (1 Corinthians 1:20–21). God has been pleased to communicate his grace to the world through the folly of the cross.

Worldliness for the Christian, therefore, is to abandon the horror and foolishness of the cross and instead to offer in its place a more sophisticated message or cool image. Sweet reason and moderation will want to dilute the Christian message so that the cross will lose its offence.

Few of us enjoy being regarded as fools, obscurantist, bigoted fundamentalists, or intellectual dinosaurs. To abandon the cross and offer a more palatable message can be powerfully tempting, but the Bible sees it as the folly of worldliness.

Worldly religion

Third, Paul sees "worldly religion" as a subtle cul-de-sac leading nowhere. He challenges the Colossians, for instance, not to get involved in "the elementary principles of the world" (Colossians 2:20). He asks them, "Why, as if you were still living in the world, do you submit to decrees such as 'do not handle, do not taste, do not touch'?" (Colossians 2:20–21). He warned them not to allow anyone "to take you captive to the tradition of men" (Colossians 2:8), adding, "no one is to act as your judge regarding food or drink or in respect to a festival, a new moon or a Sabbath day" (Colossians 2:16).

The very rules which some want to impose to stamp out "worldliness", Paul regards as another form of worldliness! We must always be on our guard against prescribed and imposed rules and regulations which can simply reflect the culture in which we were raised or to which we may personally have become accustomed.

Some fiercely imposed standards are far removed from the atmosphere of the New Testament where Paul says such things as, "For everything created by God is good and nothing is to be rejected if it is received with gratitude, for it is sanctified by means of the word of God and prayer" (1 Timothy 4:4–5).

Regimented and harsh legalism is absent in the New Testament. The gospel brings freedom. Instead of the imposition of detailed rules, Paul prefers to appeal to every person's conscience (2 Corinthians 4:2) and he invited other people to judge what he says (1 Corinthians 10:15). On such matters as a man's hair length, for instance, he simply says, "Does not even nature itself teach you that if a man has long hair, it is a dishonour to him?" (1 Corinthians 11:14). But no particular length is prescribed, no measurement given. How long is long? Certainly, the most recent fashions or your personal preference cannot arbitrarily dictate the standard. The Puritans, for instance, with their reputation for diligent obedience to Scripture, grew their hair far longer than modern trends. Don't duck the offence of the cross, but let's not be unnecessarily offensive about hair length!

Legalism and mission

Undoubtedly, one of Paul's motives for releasing believers from the shackles of legalism was that they might run unencumbered to evangelise the nations with a message of freedom. Legalism undoubtedly frustrates mission. We are not called to impose our cultural preferences on other nations, any more than Paul wanted to impose a Judaistic kind of Christianity on the Gentiles of his generation. We go with good news of grace and liberty.

We have no commission to impose a Western lifestyle on the nations (be it British or American). Christianity is not a Western religion reflecting Western cultural preferences and styles. Grace sets peoples free from their idols to serve the true and living God and wait for his Son from heaven (see 1 Thessalonians 1:9–10), but let each ethnic group bring its distinctive contribution, its colour, language, music and diversity. Grace teaches us to liberate the nations, not to clone them!

Crucified to the world

Paul's final cure to worldliness is the cross. "May it never be that I would boast, except in the cross of our Lord Jesus Christ," he says (Galatians 6:14). But notice that he doesn't regard "the old rugged cross" merely nostalgically or sentimentally; he boasts in the cross by which the world has been crucified to *him* and *he* to the world (see Galatians 6:14 – my italics). The cross for Paul was not merely a memory but a powerful, life-changing experience dealing the death-blow to any world-based expectations and aspirations that he might have had, including his reputation.

Having received the deathblow of the cross, we must all have dealings with the world, but must live as though we had no dealings with it. As the New International Version has it, ". . . those who use the things of the world, as if not engrossed in them. For this world in its present form is passing away" (1 Corinthians 7:31, NIV). We cannot prove ourselves not to be "worldly" by simply learning a few rules of conduct or simply retiring into a monastic lifestyle. Jesus offended the religious of his generation, demonstrating his friendship with sinners by eating and drinking with them. But he never compromised his own life of purity and innocence or let the world shape his value system.

We need a radical change of attitude and a thoroughgoing renewal of the mind. Paul encouraged the Roman Christians to present their bodies to God as a living and holy sacrifice, to refuse conformity to the world, and to be transformed by the renewing of their minds so that they might prove the will of God, what is good, acceptable and perfect (see Romans 12:1–2).

Personal devotion to God, motivated from within, replaced a list of rules imposed from without. We shall pursue this further in our next chapter.

10

Grace teaches us to say "No"

Sadly, some Christians give the impression that they are not allowed to participate in this world's pleasures. They seem to communicate that they are far from happy about the prohibitions that shape their narrow lifestyle.

This chapter opens our eyes to what grace teaches us and how it provides us with God-given motivations that set us free to prefer and choose Godliness, and say "no" from our hearts to the short-term pleasures of sin.

Grace teaches us to say "No"

"Should we apply grace or righteousness?" I was being asked a question at an open forum for leaders and this one provided a real shock to my system. The questioner explained that an unmarried couple who were living together were asking about the possibility of being baptised at his church. What should he say? The enquirer clearly saw grace and righteousness as alternatives!

When God declared the Old Covenant obsolete (Hebrews 8:13) and introduced a New Covenant, he wasn't throwing in the towel in the battle against sin; he was revealing a new and better way of overcoming it. In the coming of Christ, grace suddenly "appeared" (Titus 2:11. Greek: *epiphany* – "shone out"), not to lower the standards but to equip believers to rise to unprecedented heights.

Not that God had not always been gracious. When Moses asked for a revelation of God he was told that God's presence would pass before him and that he would reveal his name. So Moses heard "the Lord, the Lord . . . compassionate and gracious . . . slow to anger" (Exodus 34:6). God has always been gracious. However, grace was particularly displayed in Christ's coming. The law came by Moses; grace and truth came through Jesus Christ, and of his fullness we have all received grace upon grace (see John 1:16–17). Grace certainly shone out in the coming of Christ but grace doesn't come to lower the standard. It comes to motivate and enable us to live a totally new life.

Paul told Titus that the grace of God appeared instructing us to say "No" (Titus 2:11–12, NIV). The vivid translation of the New International Version arrests our attention. Saying "No" is a vital part of holy living. The downward gravitational pull of human society is so all-pervasive that if we don't learn to say "No", we will soon be in trouble. If young people don't learn to say "No", they will be quickly compromised by the opposite sex. If they don't learn to say "No", they will soon be experimenting with drugs and alcohol.

"No" is a word we must be instructed to say. It is an anti-social word. It goes against the tide. It takes courage and commitment to say it. It needs strong motivation, and grace motivates powerfully.

How does grace teach us? It begins by telling us that we are totally acceptable to God through our faith in Christ. We are justified freely as a gift. So I am a winner before I start. I am accepted before I have done anything. What a relief! How magnificent! Some would argue, "How dangerous!", but they don't understand. God starts by totally qualifying us. He will test us later, but he qualifies us first. We start accepted, qualified, justified as a gift. The righteousness of Christ is freely given to me, not only to start my Christian life but every day of my life, and he is the same yesterday, today and forever. His totally righteous life of magnificent decisions, perfect holy choices, steadfast purity in the face of fierce temptation, is freely credited to my account.

This is so encouraging that it is almost too good to be true. When I first heard the grace of God I felt like the early witnesses of the resurrection. It says of them, "They could not believe for joy." I had lived in a school of tough and zealous commitment for quite a while. Condemnation was often overshadowing me. Trying harder was the way to succeed! School reports with their oft-repeated "Could do better" and "Should try harder" had a similar ring to my understanding of how to live the Christian life.

Suddenly I saw it! God's grace covers my failure and sin and justifies me freely as a gift. What a revelation! What joy! What thanksgiving and praise! Grace instructs me first by telling me I am a winner before I start.

Purchased jewel for his brow

Then grace tells you that Jesus wants you for his very own possession, his special treasure (Titus 2:14). God has a particular and personal delight in you. He chose you from before the foundation of the world. He foreknew you and predestined you to be his own. He calls his church "My Delight is in Her" (Isaiah 62:4). God actually delights in you. He didn't save you by mistake. He didn't have to take you in a "job lot". You were not born of human will but by the will of God. He will always love and cherish you.

> Not my own but his by right
> His peculiar treasure now.
> Fair and precious in His sight
> Purchased jewel for his brow.
> He will keep what thus he sought
> Safely guard the dearly bought,
> Cherish that which he did choose
> Always love and never lose.
> Frances Ridley Havergal (1836–1879)

Next, grace teaches us about the terrible price that was paid for our salvation. Those three simple words are so unfathomable in their depth: "*He gave himself.*" Some, motivated by kindness, might give a gift, or even a fortune, but he gave himself. He gave himself to the human race. He gave himself to a motley band of followers who would deny him in his hour of need, he gave himself to Satan's hour, he gave his cheek to those who tore out the beard, he didn't hide his face from spitting. He gave himself to the full wrath of God, the total curse of the law. He gave himself without reserve, though he was appalled in Gethsemane, though he shuddered at the shocking revelation of the bitterness of the cup. He sweated, as it were, great drops of blood, pleading with his Father that if it was possible it might be taken from him. Yet he prevailed, determined to save us, and for the joy set before him endured the cross, despising the shame.

He became the centre of mocking and shame from men and demons. He gave himself to the sheer fury of a holy God who hates sin with a perfect loathing, and fierce anger. The Son of God loved me and gave himself for me.

Here is the crux of the matter (Latin: *crux* – "cross"). From the cross came the excruciating cry (*ex* – "from"; *crux* – "cross"). Was there ever a more excruciating cry than the one that pierced the heavens on that terrible day? "My God, my God, why have you forsaken me?" Grace teaches me by telling me about the price that was paid.

Grace also teaches me what a glorious goal he had in mind. He wants a people red-hot for good deeds (Titus 2:14). He wants zealots. He hates lukewarmness. He would rather we were cold or hot. Lukewarmness makes him vomit (Revelation 3:16). He wants passionate people burning with motivation and wholehearted in commitment. He gave his own life as our example. Zeal for his Father's house consumed him.

God wants us red-hot for the works that he foreordained for us. He doesn't want mere busyness or hectic activity. He has prepared handpicked works for us. Grace teaches me that he chose the works in advance and he wants me excitedly committed to doing them so that he can finally, enthusiastically, receive me to his eternal kingdom with the glorious words, "Well done, good and faithful servant."

It's a passing age

Finally, grace teaches me that this world can be viewed simply as "this present age" (Titus 2:12). It is not permanent; it is just what's taking place now for a short while. We only live briefly, like a flower that buds, opens, fades and quickly falls, so the very world itself is short-lived. This age is passing away. Grace opens my eyes to that reality. If I thought this life was going to last forever I might live differently, but I know it's brief. Eternity awaits. The new heavens and the new earth are ahead.

I often travel internationally and stay briefly in other countries. Often I don't fully unpack my case. I don't learn the language. Sometimes, if it's a particularly brief visit to continental Europe, I don't even change any money or adjust my watch. Walking down the street, I probably look like anyone else, but actually I don't belong! I don't fully identify. In a few days or hours I won't be there; I'll be flying home again. I belong elsewhere!

Grace teaches me not to get my roots down too deeply in this temporary scene. Grace teaches me that it's easy to say "No" when I am not really part of the culture; I am a visiting alien; my citizenship is elsewhere.

Not only do I not belong, I am eagerly anticipating another "appearing". Grace has "appeared" (Titus 2:11) but soon the "glorious appearing of our great God and Saviour" will take place (Titus 2:13). This full revelation will soon burst upon the world. He will come to be glorified in his saints and to be marvelled at among all who have believed (2 Thessalonians 1:10).

Saying "No" to the world, the flesh and the Devil seems to make good sense when grace instructs me about all these things. When I am told that actually I am an heir of eternal life (Titus 3:7), I tend to lose interest in the "here today and gone tomorrow". I feel like fixing my hope on the grace that's coming to me at the revelation of Jesus Christ. As Jim

Elliott, the young American missionary martyr, said, "He is no fool who gives up what he cannot keep, to gain what he cannot lose."

People instructed by grace will make decisions that come from their renewed heart. Grace teaches *us* to say "No". This is very different from reluctantly yielding to an external law, which forcefully and unyieldingly communicates, "Thou shalt not!"

Sadly, when Christians have not discovered the riches of grace, they often give the impression that they are externally bound and even reluctant in their law-keeping. They can communicate to the unbeliever that they are simply not allowed to do what worldly people do and that "Christians simply don't do those sort of things" – though perhaps betraying a hint that they only wish they could. Often, our failure to demonstrate wholehearted and joyful acceptance of God's holy standards communicates to the onlooker that we are unhappy and frustrated people chafing against the imposition of religious rules, which we are obliged to keep. The transformation which grace accomplishes is altogether different. Grace persuades and instructs us inwardly. It opens our eyes to the wonders of God's kindness and the attractiveness of God's ways.

Grace does not drop the standards and fudge issues. Grace does not tell us to forget about righteousness because God has changed the rules and accommodated our weakness, turning a blind eye and making do with compromising Christians. In stark contrast, grace liberates, grace instructs, grace calls us higher and enables us to live an altogether different life flooded with gratitude and revelation and the enjoyment of the presence of the Holy Spirit. Jesus was not kidding when he spoke of a righteousness that would surpass the righteousness of the Pharisees and scribes. His kingdom brings in a different righteousness altogether.

11

The grace of discipline

Now that you are free from law, and can relate directly to God as your heavenly Father, it is of great importance that you take his training seriously. He receives you as a son and will deal with you appropriately, providing discipline where necessary.

In this chapter we will show that the Father's purpose is to train you into his family likeness. Some of his instruction is tough, but his goal is to bring you to a maturity that will please him and bring you fulfilment.

How the eagle treats her young will provide us with a helpful illustration.

The grace of discipline

Having been set free from your childhood submission to the law and having received full rights as a son (Galatians 4:5, NIV), Paul urges you not to submit again to your past masters. Now that you enjoy the full privileges of sonship, you are invited into a direct relationship with God as your Father. You no longer have to keep your eye on the child-minder who previously kept you in check.

Who then will keep you in check? God in his great love will act as a true Father and provide his own discipline. Indeed, if you know nothing of God's fatherly discipline you have reason to question whether you are a true son of God. "What son is there whom his father does not discipline?" the writer to the Hebrews asks (Hebrews 12:7).

Discipline is not something that many will volunteer for. I can still remember the apprehensive queue of boys at my old school lining up outside the headmaster's room to receive his particular form of discipline.

God deals with you as sons

The writer to the Hebrews urges his readers to receive God's fatherly discipline with gratitude and understanding. First, he wants them to realise that in being disciplined they are being treated as sons: "God deals with you as with sons" (Hebrews 12:7). He goes on to argue that discipline is actually a proof of sonship. A father has no responsibility for every child in his street. He feels no obligation to correct a neighbour's child (though he might like to do so!) but he does feel parental responsibility for his own. It is a mark of sonship to experience discipline. It is proof that you belong!

The Lord "punishes every one he accepts as a son" (Hebrews 12:6, NIV). Though you have received full rights of sonship through the cross, this does not mean that you have become mature overnight! You have a new standing in God's presence through his grace, but God still has work to do in you. It could be said that God loves you as you are, but he loves you too much to leave you as you are! He wants mature sons and daughters and you have to be trained into that maturity through discipline.

The writer to the Hebrews is honest in saying, "No discipline seems pleasant at the time, but painful" (Hebrews 12:11, NIV). There are times of difficulty when you must resist the Devil and he will flee. When you are experiencing an enemy attack you should discern it, standing firm in faith and refusing his onslaught. However, when as a Christian you go through painful, unpleasant circumstances, you have to ask yourself if perhaps God is at work in your life. It may be that the pain you are currently experiencing is the result of unforeseen circumstances or even other people's sin, but it is important that, as a child of God, you consider the possibility that this is a God-appointed training session.

It was very evident, for instance, that Joseph's sufferings were the outcome of his brothers' envy and jealousy. They were the human instruments but we are told that God meant it for good. God was working behind the instrumentality of men, even in their sinfulness. Joseph, his chosen servant, was being disciplined and prepared for great future responsibility.

Training is tough, but "afterwards it yields the peaceful fruit of righteousness" (Hebrews 12:11). Discipline has purpose. It produces an "afterwards" which should include good fruit. Your responsibility is to receive discipline well and to be trained by it. Sadly, it is very possible to fail to be trained and therefore gain nothing from the painful experiences that you may pass through.

First, you must never forget that you are God's beloved son or daughter and are therefore being treated as such. You are not merely a plaything of circumstance and random events. You are in your Father's hands. He is making things work together for your good. No one can pluck you from his hand and he watches over your days. So if difficult things cross your path, you must stop and remember your identity and not be confused.

Don't make light of it or see it as too heavy

Then, as a son, you must "not make light of the Lord's discipline" (Hebrews 12:5, NIV). Don't shrug it off as though nothing were happening. Don't ignore the season you are passing through. This is no time for a cavalier attitude or a careless "Hallelujah anyway" approach. Beware of missing the point. I remember boys coming out of the headmaster's study, having been whacked, turning to those waiting their turn and arrogantly claiming, "Didn't feel a thing!" Sadly, one would have to add, "Didn't learn a thing!" Nothing is gained by making light of the Lord's discipline.

The writer then adds, "Do not lose heart when he rebukes you" (Hebrews 12:5). This opposite reaction is just as dangerous. Don't throw in the towel. Don't give up. Don't complain that God is against you or has forgotten you. It's so easy to hit the self-pity button. When you give up, you learn nothing. Little children often cry, "It's not fair" or "You don't love me." Some Christians say, "I'm just hopeless. Nothing works out for me."

You must approach the tough experiences you encounter with maturity and demonstrate a humble and teachable attitude. The season of suffering is meant to produce fruit and you are promised that it will for those "who have been trained by it" (Hebrews 12:11). If you miss the training aspect you gain nothing, indeed suffering does not automatically produce holiness and sanctification. It can produce the very opposite. Bitterness and misery often characterise those who have experienced tragic circumstances. The writer presents you with two alternatives – grace or bitterness. He says, "See to it that no one comes short of the grace of God and that no root of bitterness springing up causes trouble and by it many are defiled" (Hebrews 12:15).

When you go through hard times, bitterness is waiting at the door, offering you fellowship. He tells you what a terrible time you have had, how cruel some people have been, how unjustly you've been treated. If you yield to his offer of companionship, a root will grow in your soul as a result of which many will be defiled. Bitterness is a vile weed. It puts its roots down deep into people's personalities. Not content to disfigure just one soul, it grows up searching for others who might be willing to draw near and find themselves defiled. As a result, the only way to withstand bitterness is to make sure that you don't come short of the grace of God. Grace, like an effective fire extinguisher, can overwhelm the power of bitterness. Like a modern weedkiller it can go to the root and destroy its power. But you must deliberately obtain grace. You must make a specific choice to refuse bitterness, not once but many times. Bitterness will repeatedly knock at your door and you must always send grace to answer it.

Again, Joseph proved such an exemplary figure. He refused to be bitter towards his brothers in spite of their cruelty towards him. He looked to God and believed in his greater providential purposes. He gave absolute, free forgiveness to his brothers and kept his own soul clear and unspoiled. Nor were any others defiled. No Egyptians were in danger of hearing from Joseph how wickedly his brothers had treated him. He gave them such honour and received them with such evident and unmixed joy that no suspicions arose. He had obtained grace and God's grace was sufficient for him.

Down through the centuries, great servants of God have discovered the secrets of drawing on this magnificent grace. Madam Guyon was an outstanding example. Unjustly imprisoned, she composed the following song:

> Strong are the walls around me,
> That hold me all the day;
> But they who thus have bound me
> Cannot keep God away.
> My very dungeon walls are dear
> Because the God I love is here.
>
> They know who thus oppressed me,
> 'Tis hard to be alone;
> But know not One can bless me
> Who comes through bars and stone.
> He makes my dungeon's darkness bright
> And fills my bosom with delight.
> T C Upham, *The Life of Mme Guyon*,
> James Clarke & Co.
> *Used by permission.*

In her loneliness she refused to be bitter. Grace more than met her needs and as a result she has inspired believers for centuries.

Family likeness

In conclusion you are told, "Therefore, strengthen the hands that are weak and the knees that are feeble and make straight paths for your feet, so that the limb which is lame may not be put out of joint, but rather be healed" (Hebrews 12:12–13). It seems that your training session had a particular purpose. Your trainer had observed some lameness in your walk. A fault was apparent to him. He realised that measures must be taken to bring healing to the lameness, so a training programme was prepared with that goal in view. There would, however, be a risk factor. Instead of the limb being healed, it might be put out of joint. In other words the result, instead of providing the intended healing, would be a condition worse than before.

How vital therefore, that you handle your Father's discipline well. How crucial that you don't come short of the grace of God. "God disciplines us for our good, that we may share in his holiness" (Hebrews 12:10). His goal is glorious – sharing the very holiness of God! God wants you to carry more family resemblance, taking on more likeness of your Father. Therefore whom the Lord loves he disciplines.

If you have never experienced God's discipline in your life, it is possible that you are not really a son. You may attend church, but you may not yet be a child of God. If you are his child, you almost certainly will have experienced the reality of what this chapter describes.

In his wonderful grace God will discipline you for your good. Indeed, many could testify that in such seasons they learned more than at any other time regarding their own dependence on God and his phenomenal kindness. They also learned more of his specific love for them. Lessons learned in the midst of God-ordained trials and pressures are to be highly valued and not forgotten. They are proofs and evidences of his grace towards you. Your responsibility is to receive these difficult times with faith and confidence, knowing that God is for you. Never entertain the enemy's lies that God has forgotten you, but celebrate the fact that God's goal is to transform you to the image of his Son.

The eagle's nest

In his great prophetic song (recorded in Deuteronomy 32), Moses paints a dramatic picture of the eagle that stirs up its nest and hovers over its young until they fall from that nest high up on the rock face. One can imagine the shock experienced by the young eagles when their parent seems to have undergone a complete change of character. Instead of the normal loving, caring figure who always brings their food and cares for their every need, the parent suddenly seems careless, or maybe even callous. Not content with breaking up the nest, she actually pushes them out.

Perhaps it would help to ask a few questions such as, "Who is stirring up the nest?" Is it a hostile predator with evil intent? So often, when we face problems, we jump to the hasty conclusion that we are under enemy attack. The Devil and his minions are blamed.

On this occasion, however, the enemy is not responsible. The parent is making life uncomfortable.

Note also that she is only stirring up one nest. She is not on a binge of random nest-destruction, but concentrating exclusively on her own. When they go through difficulties, some believers ask serious questions about whether they truly are Christians. Can God really be my Father if he lets this happen to me? Can God really love me and yet not protect me? Do I really belong to God's family? Maybe God has given up on me. But in our eagle illustration, the parent eagle only stirs her own nest. Being shaken is not proof of God's indifference but a guarantee that you are in the family and getting the family treatment!

When does she inflict this horrific experience on her young? Surely not when they are too young, before wings and feathers are fully formed, but maybe sooner than we would have expected. My guess is that she stirs up the nest when she instinctively knows that it would be dangerous for them to stay as they are any longer.

The young eagles may not share her view, since they may quite enjoy the breathtaking view from the nest, high up on the rocks, and also the predictability of the safe arrival of daily food that you don't even have to order on the

Internet. It just turns up, lovingly prepared and sufficient for every need. What could be more cosy and comfortable? Who needs change? Maybe your brother or sister eagles are a bit pushy at times, but that's a small price to pay for all the comforts and bonuses of being a nest-bound eagle with a guaranteed daily menu and a great view.

Into this delightful and complacent lifestyle comes the discerning eye of the parent eagle. It's time to shake the nest! She knows that it is dangerous for them to stay still any longer. The parent sees hidden hazards long before the young. She hovers over them, she stirs up the nest, she makes it difficult to stay still any longer. Maybe the young are wondering what has got into her? Did she get out of the nest on the wrong side this morning?

No, this is no failure on the parent's part. She knows exactly what she is doing. Of course, the young could misinterpret the turn of events. As twigs from the nest disappear over the edge of the cliff and hurtle down the rocks, fear would not seem unreasonable or misplaced.

Don't you care?

Fear is often our greatest enemy at times of parental discipline and training. Has God forgotten me? Why is God letting this happen? The Israelites accused Moses of bringing them into the wilderness in order to kill them, and the disciples, caught in their stormy night at sea, asked, "Don't you care that we are perishing?" Fear ruled the situation. Terror dominated the scene.

Why are believers subjected to such experiences? Why are young eagles pushed out of their nests, perched as they are high on the cliff edge? There is one simple answer. Eagles are actually born "in heavenly places". They didn't have to work to get there. They did not climb the steep rock face. The eggshell opened and they were born there! It is all that they have ever known. But the fact remains that eagles are meant to fly! They are born to rule the sky. They are majestic on the wing. They are not turkeys or squawking hens. They are not made for passive, stagnating nest-dwelling.

They need to grow into their destiny and the parent knows just what is called for – nest-bashing!

But don't fail to see the tender side so beautifully on display. When going through such times we may want to ask where the Lord is. Why is my path hidden from God? The fact is that at this precarious time, the eye of the parent eagle is never more sharply focused on her young.

Formerly, she had often flown long distances in search of food. Now, as she breaks the nest and stirs them up, she is diligently watching every move. Not an absent, indifferent parent but, like God, a very present help in trouble.

As they fall and experience the first aerobatic tug on their wings, the young find to their delight that she catches them on her pinions (Deuteronomy 32:11). Underneath are the everlasting arms (Deuteronomy 33:27). She hasn't abdicated her responsibilities at all. She is training them for life and purpose, and jealously watching over them in the process. Soon they will fly like she does. Soon they will share her mature skills and mount up, displaying the family likeness.

As a believer, you have also been born seated with Christ in the heavenlies, with a capacity for flight. But without discipline and training you will never reach your full potential. Dull predictability and inertia based on unchanging nest-life will undermine your true identity, so learn to embrace the hardship as a good soldier and be trained by the grace of discipline so that you can share Christ's robust and triumphant holiness.

12

Keep in step with the Spirit

External law cannot transform you, so God provides a new heart and a new spirit. He puts his desires within you and gives you new appetites and preferences. His Spirit gives new life and freedom and replaces the "oldness of the letter" in your experience.

In this chapter we shall also notice that the empowering presence of God's Spirit does not mean that we no longer need instructions or exhortations. We need not fear that New Testament exhortations are putting us "back under law". Until "the perfect comes" we will need not only to yield to our inner desires, but also to the appeals and commandments of Scripture, in order to become winners over the world, the flesh and the Devil.

Keep in step with the Spirit

Jeremiah, the weeping prophet, is renowned for his dire warnings to Israel and for prophesying that they would be expelled from the Promised Land. The one ray of light that contrasted with his dismal forebodings was the great promise that in the future God would make a new covenant with his people. In contrast with the imposition of an external law, he was going to relate to them inwardly: "I will put my law within them and in their hearts I will write it" (Jeremiah 31:31–33).

Ezekiel proclaimed a similar message, "I will give you a new heart and put a new spirit within you and will remove the heart of stone from your flesh and give you a heart of flesh. I will put my Spirit within you and cause you to walk in my statutes" (Ezekiel 36:26–27).

The law engraved in stone had failed to produce holiness in Israel and, after repeated prophetic warnings, they experienced the ultimate judgement – banishment from the land. God, however, didn't wash his hands of his people or his purposes. He confidently began to forecast a new day and a new covenant that would succeed. Guilt, failure and death would ultimately be overcome. A valley of dry bones would be transformed into an exceedingly great army. This would come about by a fresh activity of the Spirit of the Lord (see Ezekiel 37). More was needed and now more was promised in the shape of a new covenant.

A new covenant

Centuries passed until a memorable night when Jesus of Nazareth gathered his disciples to celebrate the Passover and simply but majestically stated, "This cup, which is poured out for you, is the new covenant in my blood" (Luke 22:20). His blood would soon be shed to establish God's new way of relating to his people. Jesus, our Passover, would lay down his life. As John the Baptist had said, "Behold the Lamb of God that takes away the sin of the world," adding, "I baptise you with water; but one is coming who is mightier than I . . . he will baptise you with the Holy Spirit and fire" (Luke 3:16).

John the water-baptiser introduced Jesus in these two ways – the sin-bearing Lamb and the Holy Spirit-baptiser. It was as if he said, "I plunge you into water, but one is coming after me who will plunge you into holy power"! John was the herald of the great day of the coming of God in power. On one of the great feast days Jesus stood and promised that the coming of the Holy Spirit would be like rivers of living water flowing from the innermost being of those who believed in him.

In the upper room Jesus drew his disciples' attention to this theme more than any other: "The Spirit of truth is coming. He will be in you" (see John 14:16, 17). The Holy Spirit would fortify them from within. It would be as though Jesus was personally with them again, but this time not as an external friend but as one within them as their guide, teacher, motivator, energy-supplier, boldness-imparter and life-transformer. They were not to leave Jerusalem until they were clothed with power from on high and received the promise of the Father (see Luke 24:49).

On the Day of Pentecost the explosive event took place. A noise from heaven like a mighty rushing wind filled the whole house. Fire rested on each of them and they were all filled with the Holy Spirit. Joy, freedom, authority, boldness and love knew no bounds. They were transformed people.

Thousands were saved and added to the new, rapidly growing community of believers. Generosity between them exceeded anything that the Old Testament law had required. God's love was poured out in their hearts by the Holy Spirit who had been given to them. God's overwhelming, divine, measureless love flooded them to such a degree that they no longer regarded things as belonging to themselves. No more dutiful tithing and carefully measuring a tenth; they freely shared everything as any had need. Their experience of the Spirit revolutionised them from the inside. They might have been dismissed as mere drunks by their enemies, but their inner transformation surpassed the realm of emotion. It touched their pockets! They were genuinely changed people. They had been plunged into a power that released them from normal attitudes to money and self-interest and made them phenomenally generous and liberated.

Paul explained to the Roman church that this was what the New Covenant was all about. The coming of the Spirit in power in people's lives would release them to live a new lifestyle altogether. What the law could not accomplish in us because it was hampered by our flesh, God accomplished through condemning sin in his own Son in our place, so that the law's requirement might be fulfilled in us who did not walk according to the flesh but according to the Spirit (see Romans 8:3–4).

The Spirit of life

The Spirit is, therefore, the key to your new relationship with God. Although the external authority of the law has come to an end, that does not mean that the goal of righteousness is abandoned. On the contrary, what the law could not do because sin was stronger than law, Christ and the Spirit have now accomplished. The coming of the Spirit marks the end of the time of the law's role towards the believer. So now you serve in newness of the Spirit, not in oldness of the letter (Romans 7:6).

Christ has borne in his body the condemnation that you deserved so that you might be set free, not only from your guilt, but also from the age of "law-keeping" as the basis of a relationship with God. Now a new "law" works inside you. "The law of the Spirit of life in Christ Jesus has set you free from the law of sin and death" (Romans 8:2). As Ezekiel had promised, the coming of the Spirit brings life into what was formerly dead. The Spirit releases you from the tyranny of sin by his powerful indwelling. Paul wants you to appreciate not only Christ's great work of crushing condemnation through his cross, but also his life-imparting power that comes to you by the indwelling Spirit who, by his power, fulfils in you what the outward law could not fulfil.

New Testament believers were essentially people of the Holy Spirit and were characterised by the Spirit's presence and power. When Paul encountered the small group at Ephesus his opening question was not, as ours might have been, "Are you Christians?" or "Have you been saved?" He asked, "Did you receive the Holy Spirit when you believed?" (Acts 19:2). Similarly, when challenging the Galatians about their experience, Paul did not ask, "Were you saved by the works of the law or by hearing with faith?" He asked, "Did you receive the Spirit by the works of the law or by hearing with faith?" (Galatians 3:2). His concern was that they were now a Spirit-empowered people and this was their essential identity. Again in 1 Thessalonians 4:8, he does not refer to "the God who saves you" but the "God who gives you his Holy Spirit". This is the kind of God he is. The Holy Spirit was not only given to the apostles to enable them to preach powerfully; he also empowered the believers to receive the word in much tribulation "with the joy given by the Holy Spirit" (1 Thessalonians 1:6). The Holy Spirit inspired their joy in the midst of persecution.

Whereas Moses' congregation in the wilderness was characterised by murmuring, grumbling and complaining, the church of Jesus Christ was known for being filled with the Holy Spirit and joy.

Christ has done what the law was incapable of doing. Sin's stranglehold on our lives has been broken by the power of the indwelling Spirit. Now our responsibility is to obey what Gordon Fee calls "the ultimate imperative", namely to "be filled with the Spirit" (Ephesians 5:18). He is God's change agent. He fulfils in us the promise of the New Covenant. The Old Covenant is now declared "obsolete" by the writer of the epistle to the Hebrews (see Hebrews 8:13). We are in a new day of grace that carries the promise, "Walk by the Spirit and you will not carry out the desires of the flesh" (Galatians 5:16). This is not an exhortation or an appeal to us to try and be holy. It is a statement of fact; Paul's categorical promise!

Enjoying a constantly Spirit-filled life, new energy will produce the fruit of love within us. God's love is poured out within our hearts by the Holy Spirit who has been given to us (Romans 5:5). Douglas Moo calls this "an abundant extravagant effusion" (Douglas Moo, *The Epistle to the Romans*, NICNT, Eerdmans, 1996). Such a God-given effusion is a powerful life-changing force.

Paul is plainly declaring that in the new day, where law observance was no longer the way to live the godly life, God's gracious gift of the Spirit was sufficient and adequate to accomplish his purposes in his people. As Thomas Schreiner says, "Paul eschews the kind of detailed regulations found in the Mishnah. Instead, he believes the Spirit empowers and strengthens believers so that they can please God. He announces our freedom in Christ, avoiding casuistry and rule-oriented ethic" (Thomas R Schreiner, *Paul,*

Apostle of God's Glory in Christ, IVP, 2001).

The perfect has not yet come

Having established this essential basis of new covenant life empowered by the Spirit, Paul was not slow to give instructions and commands to the young churches he had formed. Certainly, the secret of their success was the new infusion of life that they had enjoyed. They were essentially people of the Spirit. The promised day of outpouring had come. Nevertheless, Paul knew that the perfect had not yet come (1 Corinthians 13:10). We do not live in an ideal society, but still wait for the new glorified earth and the new glorified bodies that we have been promised. We have this treasure in earthen vessels. We battle with the world, the flesh and the Devil, so, since we still live in imperfect conditions, instructions, exhortations and even commandments are still required and given by the apostles to the churches.

You might argue, "If we are under grace, what do you mean by commandments? Isn't this placing us back under law?" Definitely not!

All New Testament exhortations spring from a basis of grace and are the outworking of our new life in Christ. It is "because of the mercies of God" that Paul exhorts us "to present your bodies a living and holy sacrifice, acceptable to God which is your spiritual service of worship. And do not be conformed to this world, but be transformed by the renewing of your mind, so that you may prove what the will of God is, that which is good and acceptable and perfect" (Romans 12:1–2). In view of all that God has done for you, you are exhorted to respond in a spiritual or rational way. New converts do not instantaneously understand what is pleasing to God. Their thinking must be renewed and informed by truth so that they can comprehend and respond appropriately.

Similarly, Paul does not impose a set of rules on the Philippians but prays for them that their love may abound still more and more in real knowledge and discernment so that they may approve the things that are excellent (see Philippians 1:9–10). As D A Carson says, "Paul refuses to set up an arbitrary set of checkpoints against which Christians are to measure themselves; he refuses to erect hoops through which believers must jump. Rather, he simply prays to his heavenly Father and asks him that these believers may pursue what is best" (D A Carson, *A Call to Spiritual Reformation*, Baker, 1992).

We are not on autopilot

Exhortations and appeals always follow on from declarations of truth about our new identity in Christ. It is because of what God has done in us by his Spirit that we are enabled to respond wholeheartedly to these appeals, but we must note Thomas Schreiner's warning: "Life in the Spirit cannot be reduced to autopilot or cruise control and although the believers in Galatia received the Spirit by faith, Paul is concerned that they may depart from their first steps (Galatians 3:1–3). Apparently, believers need admonitions to live by the Spirit" (Thomas R Schreiner, *Paul, Apostle of God's Glory in Christ*, IVP, 2001). Paul did not believe that exhorting believers contradicted the reality of the Spirit in their lives or put them back under law.

Note how Paul addressed the particular sin that shamed the Corinthian church. It would have been very easy for Paul to quote the law to them. He could have said, "Do you not know the seventh commandment, 'You shall not commit adultery'?" Instead, he was consistent with his New Covenant convictions and used a different approach, "Do you not know that your bodies are members of Christ?" and "Do you not know that your body is a temple of the Holy Spirit?" (1 Corinthians 6:15, 19). In New Covenant terms it was not simply that a God-given law had been broken, but that the very temple or dwelling place of God had been desecrated. How can someone who is one spirit with Christ become one flesh with a harlot? (see 1 Corinthians 6:15–17).

Certainly, the New Testament believers were aware of commandments that were appropriate to their new standing as saints (God's new "holy ones"). They were to walk worthy of their calling. This was not a matter of ever returning to Old Testament laws such as being circumcised, as the Judaisers were suggesting. In fact, Paul made the remarkable statement, "Circumcision is nothing and uncircumcision is nothing, but what matters is the keeping of the commandments of God" (1 Corinthians 7:19). For Paul, returning to such things as circumcision was the ultimate mistake. In Philippians 3, Paul reserves his harshest criticism for the circumcision party. Calling them literally "the mutilation", he regards them as "dogs" and "evil workers" to be avoided at all costs. Paul argues that we are the true circumcision who worship or serve by the Spirit of God, who boast not in law-keeping but in Christ Jesus, and who put no confidence in the flesh (see Philippians 3:2,3).

Undoubtedly, all Christians, no matter how mature, need specific instructions both on what to avoid and on what to pursue in the Christian life. Having exhorted the Ephesians to be filled with the Holy Spirit, Paul continued to apply specific commandments illustrating the outworking of that lifestyle.

It is of the utmost importance, however, that in this grace-filled life we must still insist that love is the heart and soul of Paul's instruction. All the commandments of the law can be summed up in loving one's neighbour (Romans 13:8–10, Galatians 5:14). Having said that, Paul's exhortations give some parameters as to what this love-filled life looks like. If specific commands were unnecessary there would be no need for exhortations. All that Paul would need to say is simply, "Be loving". Further specifics are given because it is extraordinarily easy to deceive ourselves about what true love looks like. Particular commands give shape and substance to the call to love. The essential imperative to "be filled with the Spirit" (Ephesians 5:18) is nevertheless followed by clear instructions on submission and sacrifice on the part of wife and husband respectively (Ephesians 5:22–28).

A godly life is the fruit of the Spirit (Galatians 5:22–23), the result of the Spirit's work and power in the life of the Christian. Believers overcome the flesh and the power of the law by walking in and being led by the Spirit (Galatians 5:16,18). Triumphing over envy and pride comes by keeping in step with the Spirit (Galatians 5:26). Only through the work of the Spirit can the believer keep what is commanded. So being under grace and not under the law does not imply freedom from exhortations or commands. Life in the Spirit and the freedom of the Spirit are not quenched by commands. Instead, commands are compatible with life in the Spirit.

Spirit-filled Christians who are enjoying God's grace still need to be exhorted and will need such exhortation until "the perfect comes". There will come a time when we live in glorified bodies on a glorified planet, when all that defiles and Satan himself will have been destroyed. Then there will be no need for exhortation. There will be no enemies such as the world, the flesh and the Devil, and we shall be able to do what Augustine suggested, namely "Love God and do what you like". But until the perfect comes we shall need exhortation and must not fear it or regard it as legalism.

Our next chapter, dealing with the grace of giving, will provide us with an example of the essential foundation of grace and also the apostolic method of grace-based exhortation to produce the fruit that God desires in his church.

13

The grace of giving

This chapter introduces an example of how the grace-filled life actually works in daily practice and where apostolic exhortation plays its part.

Grace also leads us into the exciting adventure of faithful giving, and of proving the goodness of God and his ability to always make grace abound to us so that we are always sufficient for every good work.

The grace of giving

Grace by its very nature overflows – more a gushing river than a stagnant pond. The evidence that we have been touched by grace is the transformation that it brings to our lives. Once we have felt its releasing power we cannot remain unchanged.

An amazing outpouring of grace took place in Jerusalem on the Day of Pentecost. Crowds gathered for the feast day, as they had a few weeks earlier for the Passover when they had turned on Jesus and cornered Pilate into crucifying him – the greatest act of wilful rebellion in world history. You could imagine the angels wondering how God's punishment would be poured out on the guilty.

I am reminded of an Old Testament event when Moses climbed Mount Sinai and in his absence Israel demanded that Aaron made a golden calf for them to worship. When Moses returned carrying the tablets of the Old Testament, the rebellion was quickly and thoroughly judged. Three thousand died in a single day.

Now Israel had not rejected Moses and made a golden calf; they had crucified the Lord of Glory and murdered their Saviour! What would God's response be to such gross wickedness? The disciples did not come down from the upper room as messengers of God's awful judgement. Instead, they proclaimed a gospel of grace and 3,000 were saved! People deserving judgement were freely forgiven and flooded with the Holy Spirit's presence.

Great grace was on them all and they were transformed to such a degree that they relinquished their exclusive right to their own possessions and shared with others wherever needs were apparent. As a result, there was not a needy person among them. An outpouring of grace resulted in a transformation of the community.

In writing to the Corinthian church some years later, Paul wanted them to enjoy a similar experience. He planned to gather an offering from them to share with the poor believers in Jerusalem. It is instructive to observe his approach, recorded for us in 2 Corinthians 8:1–9 and 9:6–15.

No commandment

First, notice what he did *not* do. He did not lay down the law and command them to give. In fact he was quite explicit: "I am not speaking this as a command" (2 Corinthians 8:8). They were not compelled to give by the apostle, nor did he say that God required it of them. The Old Testament rule that they must give a tenth was not mentioned.

On the other hand, he did not simply leave things to their own spontaneous motivation. He was not content to assume that, if the Holy Spirit wanted them to give, they would automatically respond to their own inner promptings. Paul did not share the frequently expressed British Christian attitude that it is not quite right to speak about money.

What was the apostolic method? Paul told the Corinthians about the example of others. He told them about the sacrificial giving of the Macedonian churches, but he introduced the theme in a fascinating way. First, he told them about "the grace of God which has been given in the churches of Macedonia" (2 Corinthians 8:1). Before speaking of the

Macedonians' extraordinary giving, Paul pointed to God's mighty grace given to them. It takes God's grace to free you to give extravagantly. It takes God's grace to liberate you from the natural tendency to cling to money and put your own needs first. Grace has to break through and set you free.

Grace so liberated the Macedonians that "out of the most severe trial, their overflowing joy and their extreme poverty welled up in rich generosity. For I testify that they gave as much as they were able, and even beyond their ability. Entirely on their own, they urgently pleaded with us for the privilege of sharing in this service to the saints" (2 Corinthians 8:2–4, NIV). Notice that Paul did not start by telling us how impressed he was with the Macedonians. He drew attention first to the phenomenal presence of the grace of God.

They first gave themselves

God's grace was so effective that the Macedonians didn't only give a financial gift "but they gave themselves first to the Lord and then to us in keeping with God's will" (2 Corinthians 8:5, NIV). Their response to grace was absolute devotion to God. They first gave themselves to the Lord. Until you give yourself, every pound is a battle! While you regard your possessions as essentially your own and entirely within your own prerogative, you will be vulnerable to permanent inner conflict. The Macedonians had experienced such liberating grace that they had first given themselves. When you take that step, all that is yours comes within the orbit of God's control, and giving as God directs is a matter of ongoing obedience.

Paul goes on to explain that they not only gave themselves to the Lord, they also gave themselves to the apostles. This was no token piety but a self-giving clearly demonstrated in practical devotion and contribution to the apostolic mission. They gave themselves to Paul and his co-labourers, fully identifying with them in their calling. So giving was not a private and personal matter but an appropriate outworking and joint ownership of the apostolic mission, a partnership in grace and loyalty.

In building his church, God wants us not only to give ourselves to him but to give ourselves in tangible terms to people whom he has anointed and raised up. These Macedonians gladly gave themselves to Paul, remembering no doubt how Paul had first given himself to them in sacrificial service, imprisonment and persecution as he brought the gospel to their towns.

The sharing of finance was part of the sharing of lives, even as it had been at the beginning on the Day of Pentecost. The New Covenant did not change believers' giving from 10% to 15%, or cut it to 7%. The powerful New Covenant produced a people who were joined to one another in love. The grace of God knitted their hearts so profoundly that their pockets were touched and generous sharing characterised them.

In writing to the Corinthians, Paul went on to add further motivation as he exhorted them to give. He congratulated them on many aspects of their Christian life, namely their faith, utterance, knowledge and all earnestness (see 2 Corinthians 8:7). Now he exhorted them to make sure their Christian experience was well rounded and that they "also excel in this grace of giving" (2 Corinthians 8:7, NIV). He was aiming at comprehensive Christian discipleship, so that they did not excel in some areas but drag behind in others. For Paul, the goal was well-balanced maturity.

In other words, Paul was saying to the Corinthians, you are an amazingly charismatic church. You are extraordinary in your spiritual giftings, your knowledge, your power, your words. You excel in so many gifts but don't be unbalanced! Excel in the gift of giving as well. Don't just be a tongue-speaker. Don't just be a prophet. Be a giver. Be an all-round Christian! Excel in every possible area.

The fact is that God wants you to be seriously committed to giving away money! Is that how you would describe yourself? Generosity is one of the key characteristics of a grace-filled person. Beware the danger of assessing your spirituality selectively.

Sincere love

Next, Paul says, "I want to test the sincerity of your love" (2 Corinthians 8:8). James warns us that "faith without deeds is dead" (James 2:26). It is not difficult to be caught up in a song of devotion in which you tell the Lord Jesus how much you love him, but words are cheap, words are easy.

I well remember an occasion when we were approaching a special Gift Day in my home church in Brighton. We had set ourselves a massive target and, as the time approached, the date of the Gift Day happened to closely coincide with the maturity date of an investment that I had made. As a responsible husband and father, I had invested for seven years in a government fund called a TESSA. If you invested systematically you did not have to pay tax and the capital sum accumulated well over the years. The Gift Day was approaching and so was the maturity date for my TESSA!

One Sunday, we were singing a beautiful song that begins, "I will worship with all of my heart." We came to a line which says, "I will trust you, give you everything." I joined the men in singing the male part and as the ladies echoed ". . . give you everything" I heard God speak into my spirit saying, "Thank you very much. I'll have the TESSA." God was testing the sincerity of my worship. His grace softened my heart and released my personal grip on my investment. As a church we once again hit our corporate Gift Day target as many individuals responded obediently to his promptings.

Finally, Paul referred to the ultimate motivation: "For

you know the grace of our Lord Jesus Christ, that though he was rich, yet for your sakes he became poor, so that you through his poverty might become rich" (2 Corinthians 8:9). The ultimate motivation for every believer is found in the giving of our Lord Jesus. The grace that he demonstrated at the cross wins our hearts. The one who was rich beyond all telling, all for love's sake became poor. He did not give out of his treasures but gave himself to the point where he had nowhere to lay his head. Laying aside his heavenly glory, he took on human form and humbled himself, even to the cross. The grace of our Lord Jesus comes setting us free. The price that he paid challenges all our false values and wins our hearts.

In inviting the Corinthians to give generously, Paul una-shamedly pointed to the giving of the Lord Jesus, believing that their hearts would be touched and their generosity stirred.

Jesus sat and watched

Paul does not then simply say, "So let us all give generously." He is more specific. He begins to distinguish between people. "Remember this: whoever sows sparingly will also reap sparingly, and whoever sows generously will also reap generously" (2 Corinthians 9:6, NIV). Paul is aware that as the offering is collected, people will respond differently. Generosity will be manifest here, reluctance there. Paul highlights the distinction just as Jesus did. "Jesus sat down opposite the place where the offerings were put and watched the crowd putting their money into the temple treasury" (Mark 12:41, NIV). Most ministers avert their gaze at the time of the offering. Most stewards are not staring to see how much you gave. Jesus was different. He sat opposite and watched what they were doing and distinguished between givers and evaluated their motivation. God is intensely interested in our giving.

Paul does not want people giving grudgingly or under compulsion but that "each one must do just as he has purposed in his heart" (2 Corinthians 9:7). Giving is not a casual affair. It is not a matter of loose change or what is left at the end of a demanding month. Giving has to do with purpose of heart, prioritising to put first the kingdom of God. God wants you to give what is right, not what is left!

The Scriptures urge us to keep our hearts diligently because the issues of life flow from the heart. Our giving, therefore, must be with purpose of heart. God is not glorified by reluctant offerings. Hearts that are gladdened by grace are free to give. "God loves a cheerful giver" (2 Corinthians 9:7). Giving under protest is not God's idea of joyful worship.

Sowing and reaping

Next, Paul introduces an unexpected theme. He begins to speak of sowing and reaping, promising that "he who sows sparingly will also reap sparingly and he who sows bountifully will also reap bountifully" (2 Corinthians 9:6).

We might ask what giving has to do with sowing? Surely, they are two very different activities. When you give something, it is no longer yours. Indeed, when you give, you have less than you had before. You used to have four; you gave away two; now you have only two. Sowing is an altogether different principle. When you sow you do not lose what you had, since you commit what you had to a process. If you sow something, you do so in anticipation that something will happen. In sowing you are not giving away. It does not represent loss.

Paul calls giving "sowing" and introduces a principle that anticipates the multiplication of seed and that God himself becomes involved in a supernatural activity. "Now he who supplies seed to the sower and bread for food will also supply and increase your store of seed and will enlarge the harvest of your righteousness. You will be made rich in every way so that you can be generous on every occasion" (2 Corinthians 9:10, 11, NIV).

If you are a sower, God will give you more seed. If you become actively involved in giving, God will multiply your resources that you might give more.

You might be tempted to think that this sounds like what is sometimes called "prosperity preaching", such as you might hear from an American television evangelist. The fact is that it is a totally biblical principle. Jesus himself said, "Give and it will be given to you. They will pour into your lap a good measure – pressed down, shaken together and running over. For by your standard of measure it will be measured to you in return" (Luke 6:38).

Paul adds that "God is able to make all grace abound to you, so that in all things at all times, having all that you need, you will abound in every good work" (2 Corinthians 9:8, NIV).

In speaking of abounding "grace" in this verse, it is clear that Paul is referring to God's ability to multiply finance as a result of the faithful sowing of seed through giving. The modern concept of "seed faith" popularised by American television evangelists must not be allowed to close the mind of Bible-loving believers simply because of some of the excesses associated with the application of the teaching.

Charles Hodge, the conservative reformed Bible commentator of an earlier (pre-television!) era, says of this passage, "The reference is not to inward spiritual riches but the whole context demands that Paul is dealing with worldly riches. Giving is, to the natural eye, the way to lessen our store, not increase it. The Bible says it is the way to increase it" (Charles Hodge, *The First Epistle to the Corinthians*, Banner of Truth, 1959). Hodge goes on to argue that although such teaching may seem to appeal to a carnal view of giving and receiving, this need not be the case. He says, "It is edifying to notice the difference between divine wisdom and the wisdom of men. Human wisdom says it is wrong to appeal to any selfish motive. Divine wisdom tells all who thus deny themselves that they most effectively promote their own interests", adding, "It is right to present to men the divinely ordained consequences of their actions as motives to control their conduct. It is right to tell men that obedience to God, devotion to his glory and the good of others will effectually promote their own welfare" (Ibid).

God is simply promising you that, if you will respond to his principles of seed sowing, he commits himself to multiplication and the provision of further seed for sowing. It is a biblical promise that invites faith and committed response and is the outworking of grace. God is able to make grace abound. Many could testify that their experience is thoroughly supportive of this powerful promise.

The following testimony, from a young lady in my home church in Brighton, wonderfully illustrates the point that I am making.

For quite some time I'd wanted to visit my friend, Gail Diani, in Mexico. In January I found a cheap flight departing at the end of April but didn't book it immediately. In February we had our Gift Day. I prayed about what to give and decided on a figure. Then God challenged me about it so I "upped" it a bit. I put the cheque and paperwork into an envelope, sealed it and drove off to the Sunday morning meeting.

Terry was preaching, and "giving" was naturally the theme. I thought I'd listen quite attentively to the message, agree wholeheartedly with it and then put my gift in the offering. It was a sort of "closed envelope, closed mind" mentality. You don't really need to listen hard to a message on giving if you've already decided what you're going to give. Anyway, God had other ideas.

As Terry spoke, the Holy Spirit crept up on me and suggested that maybe I could give more. By the end of the sermon I was externally my usual calm and collected self, while inwardly there was war going on. "What about Mexico?" I protested to God. "You know I haven't got any savings. If I give more there's no way I can go."

The band came together for the final song and I glanced at the offering bowls – large flowerpots stationed at the front. Everyone stood to sing and go forward with their gifts. I remained seated, wrestling over what to do, crying out to God for direction. "Is this you, me or the enemy?" I asked. "I don't want to be forced into something that you're not saying at all. Maybe I'm just getting too 'stressed out' over this. Surely, I prayed about my gift and I'm giving what I believe you told me to. So why the sense of unease? What should I do?"

People all around me were singing and streaming forward. Then God spoke. It had to be his voice because I could never have made up what he said or said it in the way he did. Frankly, I was bracing myself for the words, "Yes, I want you to give more and this is the figure – plonk!" Instead, he responded with such tenderness. "Yes," he said. "I know that I approved your gift before you got to the meeting." Then, and almost with a fatherly smile, he added, "But wouldn't it be fun to give more?" "Fun?!" I repeated, pondering the idea for a few seconds and fingering the nicely sealed envelope in my hands. "Fun? I think it would be quite fun to go to Mexico!" But God's gentle approach and gracious answer had caught me totally off guard.

Finally, I opened the envelope, wrote out a cheque for double my original figure, changed the paperwork and stuffed everything back into the envelope which I sealed as best I could. Then I got up and put my gift in the offering – probably the last person to do so. As I returned to my seat and joined in with the final song I felt happy, but I couldn't deny that there were tears in my eyes – because this sacrifice was costing me something. Needless to say, from that point on I gave up thinking seriously about going to Mexico – until the following Thursday when I received an unexpected letter from my mother.

"Daddy and I would like to give you some money for a new kitchen extension," she wrote. "We'll give you half the money this month and the rest later." What was that final figure? Was it five times what I'd given? Ten times? 20 times? No, none of these. God multiplied my gift by 22 times! So where's that number in Scripture?! Written into verses like Luke 6:38: "Give, and it will be given to you. A good measure, pressed down, shaken together and running over will be poured into your lap." My lap was brimming with provision from God and my heart with gratitude to him.

But the story didn't end there. For over 20 years as a Christian I've operated a "receive to give" principle. Whenever I'm given money, I give at least 10% of it away, and sometimes a lot more than that. Now in this case I naturally wanted to honour my parents by using their money for a new kitchen extension – which, by the way, was badly needed. But no sooner was the first instalment in my bank account than I was thinking, "Now what do I do about the tithe?" One morning, God gave me the answer. "Go to Mexico," he said. "Give Gail and her pastor's family a holiday by the sea and pay for it all."

I booked the April flight – which, to my great joy was even cheaper than before because the departure date was closer. Then I met Flor Evans, her son Johnny, and daughter Florecita in Puerto Vallarta. Her husband, John, couldn't be with us and Gail joined us later in the week. We saw the sights, sat on the beach, swam in the sea, went on boat trips, had meals in restaurants and drank massive pina colladas – all at a heavenly Father's expense. One day, Gail, the two children and I were sitting on an inflatable "banana" boat, being towed along by a speedboat. Eleven-year-old Florecita squealed with joy as we hit the waves and God spoke to me. "Wasn't it fun to give more?" he said.

At the end of the first week we went inland to Guadalajara where I saw the work that Gail is doing among the street children. At the end of week two I took all my remaining traveller's cheques to the bank, cashed them, bought everyone lunch, purchased a few presents to take home and gave the Evans family what I had left – all, that is, except for a small sum which I needed for my bus journey to the airport. When I got on the plane I had 8 pesos in my pocket – that's about 50p.

Mexico is a happy memory now and I'm rejoicing over a beautiful new kitchen extension. Both are signs of God's amazing faithfulness to me. But maybe the greatest highlight is hidden in a day when I passed another test of faith, the day when

God took me out of my comfort zone and said, "Wouldn't it be fun to give more?" – and I believed him.

As John Piper says, "Paul is saying in effect that the key to this kind of joyful, sacrificial generosity is faith in future grace. When you trust in future grace the way the Macedonians did, your life becomes a grace." He adds, "The key is to turn from the glory and guarantee of bygone grace and put your faith firmly in future grace – that 'God is able (in the future) to make all (future) grace abound to you' so that your needs are met and so that you will be able, like the amazing Macedonians, to overflow with the love of liberality. Freedom from greed comes from faith in future grace" (John Piper, *Future Grace*, Multnomah, 1995).

Paul completes the section by celebrating the fact that this ministry will glorify God. "Men will praise God for the obedience that accompanies your confession of the gospel of Christ . . . and their hearts will go out to you, because of the surpassing grace God has given you. Thanks be to God for his indescribable gift" (2 Corinthians 9:13–14, NIV).

It is God's grace from beginning to end. He favours you with amazing kindness and then makes your heart willing to abandon possessiveness and freely give. He then involves you in a process that makes grace abound, supplying ever-increasing grace to the giver and making you a channel of grace to many.

Have you allowed God's grace to set you free in this important part of your life? If not, why don't you tell God you are willing in a new way to be open to his promptings and, when he speaks to you, respond with hilarious, grace-filled giving?

14

D.I.Y.

Does grace teach us that there is really nothing left for us to do? Does God's grace simply carry us along and lead us safely home? Do we simply have to relax and let grace do the job for us?

This chapter challenges that perspective and tells us our areas of responsibility and how we can play our part and make the necessary effort to outwork God's grace in our lives.

D.I.Y.

Do it yourself? Surely, that's the very antithesis of grace! Isn't the whole point of grace rooted in the fact that I can't do it myself, I need grace to help me?

Let me end your confusion by quoting a verse very dear to people who enjoy God's grace. "Keep yourself in the love of God" (Jude verse 21). As wave after wave rolls upon the beach, so grace is always flowing to you. "Of his fullness we have all received and grace upon grace" (John 1:16). Your responsibility is simply to keep yourself in God's love. Don't wander from it. Don't take it for granted. Don't walk in the shadows when you could be in the sunshine. Don't wander into uncertainty, vulnerability and condemnation when you could be enjoying the privileges of grace and expressing continual appreciation to God for his amazing favour.

Don't question or doubt God's love or constantly ask him to prove it by repeated "Gideon's fleeces". Take responsibility for keeping yourself in God's love. Plunge into its depths and soar to its heights. Explore its breadth. Contemplate its everlasting length. He has loved you with an everlasting love. He has always loved you and will never stop loving you. Nothing can separate you from the love of Christ.

154

Since these promises are certain, keep yourself in the conscious awareness of being in the love of God.

Build yourselves up

Jude adds a further insight in a previous verse with a little more D.I.Y. advice, namely, "But, you beloved, building yourselves up in your most holy faith, praying in the Holy Spirit" (Jude verse 20). I can sometimes hear my sons huffing and puffing as they do their press-ups and lift their weights. Bodybuilding has become a popular hobby. God wants us to build ourselves up, not through press-ups but by praying in the Holy Spirit. The Holy Spirit has come to fortify and encourage us. We do not really know how to pray as we should, but the Holy Spirit himself intercedes for us. He comes alongside and inspires us (see Romans 8:26). Praying in the Holy Spirit helps us to build ourselves up.

Similarly, Paul, in making a case for private rather than public tongue-speaking, says, "One who speaks in a tongue edifies himself" (1 Corinthians 14:4), adding that in private "I speak in tongues more than you all" (1 Corinthians 14:18). So in praying "with the Spirit" (1 Corinthians 14:15) we can be involved in further D.I.Y. as we build ourselves up rather than drift into complacency. Paul determined not only to "pray with the Spirit" but also to "sing with the Spirit" (1 Corinthians 14:15). Paul engaged in Holy Spirit-inspired activity, deliberately enjoying God's empowering presence in his personal life on a regular basis. He knew that his body was the temple of the Holy Spirit where Spirit-inspired temple worship could regularly take place.

John says, "We have come to know and have believed the love which God has for us" (1 John 4:16). Do you know the love God has for you? Have you "come to know" it? Have you believed it? Sadly, many Christians cannot say with the Psalmist, "This I know, God is for me." Some not only question God's love, they even wonder if God is disposed to be against them. Like the "one talent" servant in the parable, they see their master as "a hard man" (Matthew 25:24) trying to reap where he hasn't even sown seed. He asks too much. He is impossible to please. Being a Christian is too difficult! Who can keep God happy? He asks too much. What a tragic, perverted idea! The fact is, God is for me. The Son of God loved me and gave himself for me. He makes all things work together for good for me. Jesus ever lives to intercede for me. God could not be more for me if he tried! This is breathtakingly true, so keep yourself in the love of God!

Purify yourself

The apostle John also gives us some D.I.Y. advice. Overwhelmed at the great love the Father has bestowed on us by calling us his children, he further contemplates the staggering grace that when he appears we shall be like him because we shall see him just as he is (see 1 John 3:1, 2). John adds, "Everyone who has this hope in him purifies himself, just as he is pure" (1 John 3:3). Purifies himself? Surely, we are always asking God to purify our hearts? I love the worship song,

> Purify my heart,
> Let me be as gold and precious silver.
> Purify my heart,
> Let me be as gold, pure gold.
> Refiner's fire, my heart's one desire
> Is to be holy, set apart for you, Lord.
> I choose to be holy, set apart for you, my Master,
> Ready to do your will.
> Brian Doerkson, © 1990 Mercy/Vineyard Publishing.
> *Used by permission.*

It particularly appeals to me because of its biblical balance. As we sing it, we ask God to do his part in this purifying work but we also acknowledge our own responsibility for some D.I.Y. "I choose to be holy"! Practical holiness in reality depends on your constantly making good choices. The choices you make every moment of every day reveal the kind of person you have become and increasingly shape the person you are going to be.

Your character is developed one choice at a time, as you face the diverse circumstances that come your way.

As a follower of Jesus, your choices are not to be based on pragmatism or expediency, but on pleasing the Lord. Right choices will come from inner convictions based on God's word, enlightened by the Holy Spirit and always motivated by grace rather than guilt. Gradually, winning habits are formed in your life and character. Practical choices around the house, in the kitchen, in the bedroom, in front of the television, in the workplace, at college, in relationships, in styles of speech, in the giving of forgiveness and mercy, begin to shape your life. Gradually, good choices become easier. Secret victories based firmly on biblical convictions build character. Don't simply go with the crowd or even with what seems acceptable as the Christian norm. As Jerry Bridges says, "To pursue holiness, one of the disciplines we must become skilled in is the development of Bible-based convictions. If we do not actually seek to come under the influence of God's word we will come under the influence of sinful society around us" (Jerry Bridges, *The Discipline of Grace*, NavPress, 1994).

Hidden choices that no one else knows about regarding money, use of time, television, or the Internet begin to purify your heart; things you choose as priorities and things you choose to avoid. "Having this hope," John says, "we purify ourselves" (1 John 3:3).

It's all too easy to regard the Bible as less than an authoritative guide to your personal conduct. It can be a book of wonderful promises, or fascinating stories, or quaint history. It can even be a basis for group discussion where all in the room share their perspectives of certain verses. In our postmodern generation in particular, it is not rare for Bible study groups to take the form of each person contributing what certain verses mean to them personally, without any real attempt honestly to discover what the text is actually saying and to make it our determined purpose to change our lives accordingly.

A life rooted in Bible-based convictions will tend to stand out in the crowd, even the Christian crowd! Merely to acquire a grasp of biblical doctrine without personal application to one's own life can lead to the ugly snare of pride. There is a "knowledge of the truth that leads to godliness" (Titus 1:1) but there is also a knowledge that merely "puffs up" (1 Corinthians 8:1). We need to apply Scripture to actual situations in our daily lives in order to develop genuine Bible-based convictions and thus become transformed.

We don't take such steps to earn grace from God. Rather, because grace has freely flowed to us, we choose to prioritise, aware that grace is not meant to lead to passivity but to joyful response and partnership with the Holy Spirit's inward activity.

Everything we need for life!

I vividly remember the day I first read 2 Peter 1 in the New International Version translation. The chapter had long been a favourite of mine, but I remember the particular thrill I experienced when I stumbled for the first time on the NIV translation of 2 Peter 1:3, "His divine power has given us everything we need for life and godliness." I left my desk and walked up and down the street outside repeating the phrase again and again. What a statement! What a magnificent promise to every Christian! Sometimes we find life itself is quite a challenge. Godliness seems totally out of reach. But here is a promise that he has given us *everything we need* for life and godliness! Peter goes on to speak of the precious and magnificent promises that God in his grace has given us, telling us that through them we escape the world's corruption and become partakers of the divine nature. It's a breathtaking passage!

But perhaps to our surprise it is immediately followed by some serious D.I.Y. Having received such amazing grace and breathtaking promises, we are not told simply to relax and let God do it, but instead find this surprising appeal; "For this very reason, make every effort to add to your faith . . ." (2 Peter 1:5, NIV). We need to give full weight to both phrases. First, "for this very reason", i.e. because you have been given everything you need and have such great and precious promises. God has been so good to you. He has extended such breathtaking favour to you. This is the *very reason* Peter refers to as he exhorts you to press on; not because it is so difficult and there is so little hope or help available so you will have to work hard, but because you have everything you need.

The second phrase is "make every effort". Many people drift through their Christian lives disappointed with their personal fulfilment or enjoyment. They perhaps find their way to the front of meetings at the conclusion of service after service, hoping that all their problems might be resolved by somebody praying for them. It has never occurred to them that maybe the reason for their disappointment is that they are simply not obeying this word of Peter's – "make every effort"! They have simply allowed themselves to become lethargic.

Don't be a sluggard

Again, let me emphasise that this is effort in response to overwhelming grace and God's supply of everything we need. Many Christians become despondent and disappointed simply because they are not ordering their private world. They are not making the required effort. I remember how surprised I was when I first noted in Proverbs that "the soul of the sluggard craves and gets nothing" (Proverbs 13:4). It never occurred to me that the sluggard wanted anything! The writer to the Proverbs is more discerning than I. The sluggard actually craves things! Many an "if only" drifts through the undisciplined mind of the sluggard! He wants success, but he doesn't want it enough to take action. "Making every effort" does not feature in his plans. Proverbs adds, "As a door turns on its hinges, so a sluggard turns on his bed" (Proverbs 26:14). Derek Kidner comments, "He is more than anchored to his bed. He is hinged to it!" (Derek Kidner, *Proverbs*, IVP, 1972).

Grace is not meant to produce horizontal Christians fond of their beds. Grace is meant to liberate. Grace is meant to motivate. Grace is meant to put a spring in our step and hope in our heart. Grace inspires some D.I.Y., confident that we can succeed, confident that lives previously devastated and ruined by sin but now released can be built into something for the glory of God.

Grace sets you free to take action. Beware of distorting grace and failing to grasp its wonderful liberating power. Beware the danger of passivity and blaming God for the way things seem to work out. As Dr Martyn Lloyd-Jones said,

So many people fail and become miserable and depressed simply because they have not taken themselves in hand. You will have to do it yourself. It will never be done for you, indeed, nobody else can do it for you . . . pull yourself together, don't shuffle through your Christian life, walk through it as you should do with vigour, add to it that kind of strength and power. Do not be a languid Christian who always gives the impression that he or she is on the point of swooning and fainting and might fail at any moment. (D Martyn Lloyd-Jones, *Spiritual Depression: Its Causes and Cure*, Pickering and Inglis, 1965)

I often pass through airports, extremely grateful for the moving pavements that I find there. If I have a heavy case I am happy to rest and let the machine carry me and the case along. Often, however, these wonderful automatic walkways are found within the airport, before one has collected one's luggage, so there is no need to pause. I can stride along, stretching legs that have been confined on the journey – and what a pace I can do as I take advantage of the momentum afforded me by the walkway!

I can never quite understand those who simply stand on them, though they have no heavy case to carry. Why be stationary when by making effort you gain full advantage of the provision? On those walkways even I can look pacey!

15

Grace that will not let go

A wonderful thing about God's grace is that God never gives up on us. He keeps showing his kindness and favour even when we would give up on ourselves.

This chapter takes the story of Elijah, a man like us, who plumbs the depths of despair and dejection, only to discover that, even if he makes his bed in hell, God is there for him and restores him absolutely.

Read this chapter and receive the comfort of God's unchanging grace toward you. See how kind God was to his broken servant Elijah, and be renewed in your heart as you discover some of the secrets of God's way of restoring his children.

Grace that will not let go

Elijah, we are told, "was a man just like us" (James 5:17, NIV). I must confess that he doesn't really look like us. Most of the time, that is. The Bible sometimes gives a few introductory remarks about its heroes, such as how their parents were prepared, or details of birth, or some important childhood events. Elijah, however, seemed to appear from nowhere. We have no record of his past. He just arrived. His introduction is as follows, "Now Elijah . . ." (1 Kings 17:1). He seemed to come from nowhere and then was gone again. Eventually, he disappeared into heaven. Maybe he was a spaceman or an angel! No, Elijah was a man just like us, flesh and blood, vulnerable and needy.

One moment our great hero was standing confidently on Mount Carmel calling down fire from heaven; the next he was a terrified man running for his life toward the desert. Suddenly, we can identify with him. We recognise the same human tendencies. He was transformed from a powerhouse to a puny mouse. One minute he is courageous, the next terrified; once preoccupied with God's glory, now with self-preservation; once standing firm, now running scared; once dictating history, now irrelevant; once public and visible, now hiding in the wilderness; once crystal clear about issues, now thoroughly muddled and suicidal.

So where did Elijah go wrong? Here was a man whom God had trained to bear up under pressure. "Give me your son," he had said to the widow during his training period. "Come here to me," he had said to the nation on Mount Carmel. Elijah invited pressure, so why did he suddenly collapse under it? One thing is sure: like Peter on the lake, his eyes must have drifted away from the Lord. But why?

Be angry but don't sin!

As imperfect human beings, we frequently find it hard to express righteous anger. Someone sins and we confront him, but we allow our own feelings of hostility to take over. So instead of loving the sinner and hating the sin, we lash out and condemn both. Did Elijah fall into this trap? When he challenged the priests of Baal did he slip from God's holy wrath into his own anger and frustration?

When taking your stand against modern evils, beware of adopting a judgemental spirit and working off your own personal frustrations and pet hatred. Never forget that God hates the sin but still loves the sinner. Maybe in that moment of pent-up fury Elijah momentarily took his eyes off of God.

Pride before a fall?

Elijah had spent three years concealed from the public eye. All his previous miracles were worked in private, by a hidden stream, or in a widow's humble home. Suddenly, Elijah faced not seclusion but overwhelming public triumph and vindication. An obscure prophet suddenly became the most famous man in the land.

Perhaps you have been hidden away for a while. Maybe your whole church used to meet in a living room, but now it's the biggest in town. Maybe you have begun to be used with words of knowledge or prayers for the sick. Now others are beginning to seek you out and you are getting a reputation. How are you handling it? Once you begin to gain popularity, it can easily go to your head.

Elijah's early ministry was characterised by God-consciousness. But at some point, did he suddenly become self-conscious? As he ran past the king's chariot did he think, "Hey, Ahab! Look at me. I'm motoring!" Elijah hadn't had a public ministry before, but now the spotlight was on him. Maybe self-awareness became his snare.

Was he just exhausted?

Elijah may simply have been worn out. For three years he had been living under the pressure of a drought that he had announced. Then came the emotional build up to Carmel, as the news travelled slowly across the nation without the aid of radio or television. This was followed by the emotional demands of the day itself. Finally, there was the crushing realisation that Ahab and Jezebel were untouched and unchanged. Elijah was emotionally shattered.

He probably set all his hopes on the confrontation between God and the priests of Baal. "This will turn the nation," he thought. "Everyone will worship the Lord now." Then, when Ahab and Jezebel showed no sign of repentance, the tremendous miracle seemed to be for nothing, and Elijah collapsed.

Disappointment drains you like nothing else. Let's say you decide on a special gospel outreach. Someone slaves over a dramatic script; others prepare music and Powerpoint sequences. People are praying and rehearsing hard, giving all their energies in order to make the event successful. Leaflets are printed and delivered around the neighbourhood. By the evening everything is ready. Expectations run high. The doors are flung wide – and a handful of people stroll in. As a friend of mine would say, "There's another one pouring in."

The following Sunday, the church meets as usual. "Terrific evenings, weren't they?" says everyone. "The performances were superb." But inside you are thinking, "The performances were great, but where were the audiences? We worked so hard – the babysitting, the costumes, the rehearsals. But was it all for nothing?" and if the truth be known, you are drained and deeply disappointed.

We can even be disappointed by our nearest and dearest. Lack of appreciation in marriage is very hard to bear. "She doesn't appreciate me," says the husband. "I'm out all day, coping with the pressure, making important decisions, battling to keep on top of the work. I come home exhausted wanting some time to unwind. I pick up the paper, and all she can talk about is her day."

"He doesn't appreciate me," says the wife. "I'm stuck here all day, coping with the kids, changing nappies, doing the washing, ironing, cleaning, shopping, cooking . . . 'No, don't touch that, Peter! Yes, it's pretty, Susan. James, leave that alone! It will fall over. Yes it will. It has! Now stop crying. It's only hurting a little bit. Let's kiss and make it better' . . . and after a day of this my husband comes in, flops on the sofa, picks up the paper and asks, 'Is dinner ready yet?' He doesn't care about me. He doesn't understand what I go through all day long. All he wants is my body. He doesn't appreciate me at all." Disappointment leads to bitterness and hostility. Spiritual collapse is about to take place.

Delays and dilemmas

"Hope deferred makes the heart sick" (Proverbs 13:12), as anyone knows who has waited endlessly for the house to sell or for another job to turn up.

Often you can see why things happen to you. It's raining hard. The bus shoots past the end of your road and you charge after it in hot pursuit. It stops, takes two passengers on board, and pulls away just before you arrive. The rain slithers down your neck and your face reflects a mixture of pain and despair. You stand wearily under the bus shelter where a woman joins you.

Woman: I suppose we've missed the bus.
You: Yes.
Woman: You live around here, don't you?
You: That's right. Just around the corner.
Woman: I thought so. I'm sure I have seen you go past my house to that church.
You: Yes. I'm a member there.
Woman: Oh, are you? They always seem such a happy crowd. Tell me more about it.

Suddenly, you know why you missed the bus. "It's a divine appointment," you say to yourself. "I'd miss any number of buses for a divine appointment."

When you understand the reason for things that happen, you are happy. The problem arises when you stand at the bus stop for 45 minutes and no one else turns up. Or you go to the hospital and think, "I really want to witness to the patients here", but you are so ill that it's as much as you can do to ask for a glass of water. "What's the point?" you think. Perplexity saps your strength.

Living at today's pace

Every generation encounters the pressures of life, but no generation has had to cope with stress as much as ours has. Wherever you go, you find people struggling to stay on top, packing as much as they can into every available minute.

By contemporary standards, the pace of life in Jesus' time on earth was relatively steady. If he wanted to go from one place to another, he would have to walk, ride, or sail. Today one new invention replaces another and the pace of life races forward ever faster. My father remembered the first car to be driven through our home town. He was also alive when Concorde broke the sound barrier and men walked on the moon.

Christians are trying to glorify God in the midst of this hectic experience. It has proved too demanding for many who, like Elijah, have suffered total collapse of the inner self. The computer generation has a severe headache. God views all this with tenderness and compassion.

Wilderness

Something made Elijah take his eyes off the Lord, and he fled into the wilderness, a despondent and frightened man. As he ran, his young servant's questioning eyes probed his soul. "What are you doing, Elijah? Mount Carmel was great. The fire fell, and now the rain has come. But where are we going now?" I can hear Elijah saying, "Stop looking at me like that. I can't stand it. You stay here." Elijah went on alone. Sometimes when you are running away there are eyes you would rather not look into.

Leaving his servant behind, Elijah ran into a physical and spiritual desert. He sat down under a broom tree and prayed that he might die. Having lost all sense of purpose, he felt condemned and worthless. It was then, when he was most vulnerable, that the Devil moved in maliciously and brought him to the brink of suicide.

"I might as well be dead." I wonder how many of us have ever got that far. A single parent, at the end of her rope and on the point of ending her life, holds on only because she asks, "What would happen to the children if I killed myself?" A man, unemployed for many months, reaches the stage where he wonders, "My life is totally purposeless. Why not end it all?" A young couple, in deep debt and relentlessly pursued by financiers ask, "Why are we here? We can't overcome this problem. There's no future. We might as well be dead."

The Devil comes to steal, kill, and destroy. He appears on the scene when we are at our weakest because at that time he has the greatest chance of success.

Elijah had reached rock bottom. But God did not answer his suicide prayer, nor did he condemn him for his negative attitude. Instead he treated Elijah with great understanding, tenderness and compassion.

When David was chasing the Amalekites, he and his followers came across an exhausted man in a field. They gave him food and water and then asked him why he was there. He replied, "I am an Egyptian, the slave of an Amalekite. My master abandoned me when I became ill three days ago" (1 Samuel 30:13, NIV).

Elijah's Master could so easily have done the same. If God were like us, Elijah would probably have been fired. "This is an ex-prophet. Get me Elisha!" But this is not God's style. When Elijah ran out of gas, he ran straight into grace! And grace never gives up, never ignores, and never backs off. Whenever wounded people run into grace, they run into the arms of God, who knows exactly what to do.

Natural refreshment

Before giving him spiritual instruction, God remembered that Elijah needed rest, food and time, so he gave him all three before saying a thing.

The God of the Bible "makes me lie down in green pastures . . . he restores my soul" (Psalm 23:2–3) and "grants sleep to those he loves" (Psalm 127:2, NIV). So often we can be tempted to think that relating to God is a frenzy of praying, fasting and witnessing, but that's not true. We must get to know the God who lets us lie down and gives us sleep.

Having slept soundly, Elijah woke to the touch of an angel who had prepared a meal for him. Having given the prophet a rest, God now provided nourishment. The Lord knows our body's needs. He created those needs and he fulfils them. Beware the super spirituality that looks exclusively for the supernatural answer and ignores the human side, including a good rest and nourishing food.

What is more, the meal was served by an angel. When Elijah was at the centre of God's will, he was fed with bits of food by ravens. When he ran for his life, disobedient and dejected, God did not despatch another raven but commissioned an angel. That's grace!

The Devil tells us that when we fail God, we have to suffer for it. What a lie! When we fail, Jesus does not keep us at arm's length. Instead, he comes to us. Did Jesus reject Peter after he cursed and swore that he didn't know him? No. After the resurrection, Jesus stood on the seashore and called to the disciples in the boat, "Come and have breakfast" (John 21:12, NIV). He didn't say, "Peter, you disowned me, so you can't join us." The Good Shepherd was lovingly re-gathering his flock. The disciples had been in a boat all night. They needed food and Jesus was there to give it to them. Elijah, too, had been working hard. He also needed refreshment and God was there to give it to him!

Once Elijah had slept and eaten, God did not immediately close in on him. He let him run. He gave the prophet space to get the whole thing out of his system. He was free to run and work out the tension.

Back to basics

Now that he had been refreshed by God, Elijah was no longer running aimlessly into the wilderness. He ran back to his roots, to Horeb, where God first spoke to Moses from the burning bush and made a covenant with the Israelites, giving them the Ten Commandments. Elijah was going back to his foundations.

When you are perplexed and disillusioned you must run back to the things that you know are true. Don't stay in the wilderness. Remember the foundations of your faith. Remind yourself of the things you know. Didn't Jesus say,

"I am with you always"? Isn't he the same yesterday, today and forever? Why am I allowing life to toss me around? Why am I living as though my feet were on shifting sand? I need to get back to the rock. Lots of things have happened to me that I don't understand but this I do know: God is my fortress.

You are not just following an abstract philosophy or trying to be religious. You are in covenant relationship with a God who acts and is a faithful friend to whom you can run. Don't waste time in the wilderness. Come back to your covenant-keeping God who won't fail you.

Identity and accountability

Now Elijah was ready to hear from God. He was rested and nourished and had run back to the roots of his faith. God met him with a question: "What are you doing here, Elijah?"

Elijah had come to the place where he had acknowledged that he was hopeless and helpless, an emotional mess that might as well be dead. In stark contrast, God reminded him, "No. You are Elijah. You are not a nothing. You are a person and you have a name and a history. Not only that, you are my servant. You are accountable to me, so what are you doing here?" God knew that Elijah's thoughts about himself were not true. He had run away, yes, but he was not a hopeless mess. He was God's servant, and God wanted him to see anew the dignity of his identity.

God wants you to know that you are not, as many modern philosophers suggest, simply a lot of feelings and thoughts happening one after another. A mass of feelings has no identity, but you do, and with identity comes accountability. One day, you will stand before God and give account of what you did with your life, how you used the talents God gave you. The awareness of that truth should stir you out of the complacency and lethargy that can swamp your soul after a period of discouragement.

Beware the danger of being so bound by self-pity that you lose your holy fear of God and stop serving him. For some, this medicine may be hard to take, but it will bring ultimate healing. God first gave Elijah rest, food and space, and then he asked him, "What are you doing here?" He made him face up to reality.

Intimacy

Following an awesome display of power, which tore the mountains apart and shattered the rocks, God drew Elijah near with a gentle whisper. It was not the magnificent display of power that drew Elijah to the mouth of the cave, but the soft voice that spoke to him of God's tenderness and love, reminding us of King David's testimony, "Your gentleness makes me great" (Psalm 18:35). Accountability to God must be accompanied by intimacy with him, because we will receive healing and restoration only when the two are brought together. We must hear the voice that asks, "What are you doing here?" but we must also have our ears tuned to the gentle whisper that says, "You are precious to me. I know what's happening." That woos us tenderly back into God's purposes.

God is not interested merely in how you can serve him. He wants you to hear the clear, gentle whisper, "I love you. I am for you. I know your sighing, your longings, your heartbreak. I know what you have been doing for me and how little you have been appreciated for it. I hear you when you cry out in desperation." It's this gentle whisper that melts your heart.

David said, "He rescued me because he delighted in me" (Psalm 18:19). That is one of the greatest truths in the whole Bible. God is delighted with you. When God whispers into your ear, "I am delighted with you", it's almost too much to bear.

I once looked up "delight" in the dictionary. It said "great pleasure and satisfaction" but I wasn't too pleased or satisfied with that! So I searched for it in a thesaurus. This is what I found: "laugh, smile, get a kick out of, hug oneself, rave, bask in, enjoy, wallow, have fun, exhilarate, relish, elate, thrill, ravish, intoxicate, entrance, enrapture, purr." Isn't that wonderful? When God looks at you he purrs with delight!

Have you ever fallen in love? You are in a room full of people and suddenly you realise, "She saw me!" The Bible says, "You have stolen my heart, my sister, my bride; you have stolen my heart with one glance of your eyes" (Song of Songs 4:9). Or have you ever seen parents with their first baby? "Isn't he wonderful? Doesn't he look just like me? Did you see that? That was his first smile." God purrs over his people just like that.

How do I find healing from exhaustion? It's in the gentle whisper from God, "I love you. I am delighted with you. You make my heart sing whenever I see you." That's what has overwhelmed great Christians throughout history and that's what restores your soul – a fresh experience of intimacy with God and a new revelation of his grace.

Commission

God drew Elijah close to him. Then, to complete the prophet's restoration, he gave him a job to do. He did the same for Peter, who must have thought, "After what I've done, Jesus will never trust or use me again." But Jesus, having re-established a loving relationship with his disciple, said to him, "Feed my sheep." Peter must have been stunned to hear those words repeated three times so that he really got the message, "I still want to use you." Little did he know just how greatly he would be used.

"Go back the way you came," God told Elijah (1 Kings 19:15). Then he continued, "When you get there . . ." This was no vague commission, a sort of pat on the head and a general comment, "Off you go. You'll find your way somehow." No, there was a specific job for Elijah to do. I expect that in his desolation he thought, "I'm finished. I will certainly never speak to a king again." In fact, Elijah's new commission did not consist merely of addressing one king, but of anointing two! (see 1 Kings 19:15, 16). Furthermore, while he had come to regard his life as worthless, God regarded it as worth reproducing! He was going to give him a disciple – Elisha. Some commentators say that the two prophets spent ten years working together. One failure had not destroyed all the excellent characteristics that God had built into Elijah, nor have any feelings of desolation you have recently experienced nullified all that God has taught you over the years.

"Furthermore," God was telling his servant, "you have been on your own long enough, so I am giving you a friend, someone you can care for and train to take over from you. Contrary to your expectations, your ministry is not finished. I want you to stop thinking about yourself and to start concentrating on Elisha. He doesn't know as much about me as you do. I want you to give yourself to him, praying for him and teaching him everything you know."

God has a wonderful way of working healing into weary people. If you drift away from him, he does not abandon you. No matter what you do, you are always his delightful child. His thoughts about you have never changed and never will. This is what grace is all about! And Elijah was a man just like us!

16

Future grace

Even when our present life is completed, we can anticipate yet more grace to come from our gracious God. Indeed, the best is yet in store. All limitations will be removed. Our time of groaning and yearning for completion will be over and we will enter into the fullness of his lavish grace.

The very creation itself will be set free from its futility and enter into its ultimate glorious destiny.

Knowing and anticipating these certainties releases us to live carefree lives as we make the grace of God known to our generation and go and tell the world what he has done.

Future grace

As if all that we've looked at wasn't enough, there is more grace yet to come! Peter tells you "to set your hope completely on the grace to be brought to you at the revelation of Jesus Christ" (1 Peter 1:13). God's grace will never run out even when "we have been there ten thousand years", as Newton's famous hymn has it.

So what further grace can you anticipate? The fact is that your present salvation is incomplete. We live between the ages, the "now" and the "not yet". Even *now* we are the children of God but it does *not yet* appear what we shall be (see 1 John 3:2, my italics). As John Stott says, "Fundamental to New Testament Christianity is this ambiguity of the church. We are living between the times, between what he did when he came and what he will do when he comes again, between kingdom come and kingdom coming, between the 'now already' of kingdom inaugurated and the 'not yet' of kingdom consummated" (John Stott, *Calling Christian Leaders*, IVP, 2002).

In fact, Paul speaks of our frustration in this present age, which is characterised not only by eager anticipation but also by groaning! We are groaning, waiting to be fully glorified. "And not only this, but also we ourselves, having the first fruits of the Spirit, even we ourselves groan within ourselves, waiting eagerly for our adoption as sons, the redemption of our body" (Romans 8:23).

We wait with groanings mingled with eager longings, and in that mode we are in step with the whole of creation. The creation is groaning and eagerly awaiting the full revelation of the sons of God (see Romans 8:19–22). The prospect of future grace is breathtaking. God will graciously transform us completely into the image of his glorious Son. The culmination of our salvation is not sanctification but glorification!

This will be such an epic event that the whole creation is standing on tiptoe and waiting to see the full revelation of the sons of God (see Romans 8:19). Creation is pictured as a pregnant mother, straining with birth pangs and longing for the day which will not only bring forth God's sons in all their glory but will also herald the end of creation's long night and her bondage to futility. Somehow the future of creation is inextricably interwoven with the future of the church.

Creation's pain is not regarded as merely random. Childbirth pains point forward in anticipation of a glorious future event. Jesus spoke of earthquakes and wars, describing them as the beginning of birth pains. Because of humanity's fall the very creation is itself distorted, cursed and futile, but at Christ's coming not only will we be liberated but "the creation itself will also be set free from its slavery to corruption into the freedom of the glory of the children of God" (Romans 8:21).

Though we have already been the recipients of God's glorious grace in this life, much more awaits us. What we have now is not the complete picture. Indeed, in comparison, Paul writes, "If we have hoped in Christ in this life only, we are of all men most to be pitied" (1 Corinthians 15:19). He goes on to compare our present life and our future life in the familiar terms of nature, like the seed and the full flower. At

death we shall be sown a perishable body, raised an imperishable body, sown in weakness but raised in power, sown
a natural body but raised a spiritual body. "This perishable
must put on the imperishable and this mortal must put on
immortality" (1 Corinthians 15:53).

The completion of God's saving work lies before us. Set
your hope fully on that future grace and it will set you free
from short-term fears and even bitter disappointments and
pain. Paul tells us that the sufferings of this present world
are not worth comparing with the glories that are to be
revealed in us. In comparison with eternal glory, our sufferings will seem only brief (see 2 Corinthians 4:17). Mother
Teresa is reported as saying that when we get to glory, our
life lived in this age will seem like spending one night in a
second-rate hotel!

No doubt it has been the certainty of future grace that
has released glorious faith and overcoming joy in the hearts
of the martyrs throughout the ages, as is illustrated from
this comparatively recent story from Cambodia's notorious
"killing fields".

The place was grim indeed and bore many gruesome signs
of a place of execution. A sickly smell of death hung in the
air. Curious villagers foraging in the scrub nearby lingered,
half hidden, watching the familiar routine as the family were
ordered to dig a large grave for themselves. Then, consent-
ing to Haim's request for a moment to prepare themselves for
death, father, mother, and children, hands linked, knelt together around the gaping pit. With loud cries to God, Haim began
exhorting both the Khmer Rouge and all those looking on
from afar to repent and believe the gospel.

Then, in panic, one of Haim's young sons leapt to his feet,
bolted into the surrounding bush and disappeared. Haim
jumped up and with amazing coolness and authority prevailed
upon the Khmer Rouge not to pursue the lad, but allow him to
call the boy back. The knots of onlookers peering around trees,
the Khmer Rouge, and the stunned family still kneeling at the

graveside, looked on in awe as Haim began calling his son, pleading with him to return and die together with his family.

"What comparison, my son," he called out, "stealing a few more days of life in the wilderness, a fugitive, wretched and alone, to joining your family here momentarily around this grave but soon around the throne of God, free forever in Paradise?" After a few tense minutes the bushes parted, and the lad, weeping, walked slowly back to his place with the kneeling family. "Now we are ready to go," Haim told the Khmer Rouge.

But by this time there was not a soldier standing there who had the heart to raise his hoe to deliver the death blow on the backs of these noble heads. Ultimately this had to be done by the Khmer Rouge commune chief, who had not witnessed these things. But few of those watching doubted that as each of these Christians' bodies toppled silently into the earthen pit which the victims themselves had prepared, their souls soared heavenward to a place prepared by their Lord. (Don Cormack, *Killing Fields, Living Fields*, Monarch Books/OMF International, 1997)

The restoration of all things

God's grace will not only lead us safely home, it will bring us into full glory, a salvation not only completing our individual stories and pilgrimages but putting all things in subjection to Christ. When he appears, we will not disappear but appear with him in glory! He will come to be glorified in his saints and marvelled at, among all who believe (see 2 Thessalonians 1:10).

Peter was thrilled to speak of "Christ . . . whom heaven must receive until . . . the restoration of all things" (Acts 3:21). God's great triumph is that all things are to be restored. The very creation is included in God's ultimate plan. Psalm 96:11–13 tells us, "Let the earth rejoice; let the sea roar, and all it contains; let the field exalt and all that is in it. Then all the trees of the forest will sing for joy . . .

for the Lord . . . is coming . . . to judge the earth. He will judge the world in righteousness." When he comes to judge, somehow the very creation will start applauding; the trees, the mountains, the fields will celebrate.

The Bible testifies to the full recovery of the whole creation. It will be glorious again. The earth will be full of the knowledge of the Lord as the waters cover the sea. Paradise lost will ultimately be paradise regained! "The wolf will dwell with the lamb and the leopard will lie down with the kid. The calf and the young lion and the fatling together and a little boy will lead them" (Isaiah 11:6). Alec Motyer says, "Even a child can exercise dominion originally given to man" (Alec Motyer, *The Prophecy of Isaiah*, IVP, 1993).

What a day it will be! It is so hard to imagine the new heaven and the new earth. Eye has not seen nor ear heard, nor has it entered the heart of a man what God has prepared for those who love him. But above everything else he will dwell with us. We will be his people and he will be our God. We shall need neither sun nor moon for the Lord will be our light and we shall see his face.

The longing of his people through the centuries will be thoroughly satisfied: Moses' prayer to behold his glory, the Psalmists longing to see his face, Paul's yearning to know him, for which he was willing to count all things loss. Then we shall know him even as we are known. The perfect will come. We shall see him as he is and we shall be changed to be like him.

The apostle John, exiled to the Isle of Patmos, was privileged to see the heavens opened. One extraordinary image replaced another, until at the end of our Bibles we read his wonderful words,

I saw a new heaven and a new earth; for the first heaven and the first earth passed away, and there is no longer any sea. And I saw the Holy City, the new Jerusalem, coming down out of heaven from God, made ready as a bride adorned for her husband. And I heard a loud voice from the throne, saying, "Behold the tabernacle of God is among men, and he shall dwell among them, and they shall be his people, and God himself shall be among them . . ." (Revelation 21:1–3)

We need to rethink our concepts of floating up to a spiritual realm somewhere in the blue yonder. As Bruce Milne says, "Heaven is not so much a new world 'up there' as a new world 'down here'" (Bruce Milne, *The Message of Heaven and Hell*, IVP, 2002).

Dr Martyn Lloyd-Jones also challenged the theology of an old hymn, which says,

> In the ocean of your love
> We lose ourselves in heaven above.

Instead he argued, "The redeemed will dwell in our glorified bodies, on a glorified earth, under glorified heavens" (D Martyn Lloyd-Jones, *The Final Perseverance of the Saints, Romans 8:17–39*, Banner of Truth Trust, 1975).

John saw the holy city coming down from heaven, free from all that corrupts, God himself dwelling in the midst of it. The community of heaven will touch down on the earth; God's great longing to dwell amongst his people will be thoroughly fulfilled as he comes among his own fully redeemed and fully glorified children.

As he wipes away all tears, the city of God will be flooded with his joy and peace, and "sorrow and sighing will flee away" (Isaiah 35:10). Death, our last enemy, will be thoroughly defeated and we will be with the Lord forever.

At last, God's redeemed people will enter into their full inheritance. The city of God will shine with the glory of God and at last we will be permitted to behold the radiant majesty of the presence of God. The prayer of Jesus that we might be with him where he is, "in order that they may behold my glory" (John 17:24), will be fulfilled.

Former glimpses of the glory of God, which invaded the tabernacle and the temple, will be surpassed and eclipsed. Men and women of flesh and blood could not stand in his presence as he appeared in Shekinah glory but we, in our glorified bodies, will be amazingly "at home" partaking of that glory. We shall see his throne of majesty. We shall be invited to eat of the tree of life. We shall be where the river of life forever flows and we shall see his face.

Beyond everything else, we shall be known as the bride of Christ. We are invited not simply to a "graduation service" or a "reward ceremony" but to a marriage supper! And we come not simply as witnesses or friends of the bride or groom but as participants, specially selected and delighted in, a bride without spot or wrinkle or any such thing, the joy of his heart, the reward of his suffering.

What future grace to anticipate! The Holy Spirit has been given to us as a foretaste, a guarantee, a down payment. Even now, in advance, we can touch something of the future glory, but in that hour the partial will be superseded by the fulfilment.

Grace sets you free

You can also be released to live dangerously in the present. You don't need to live as others who have no hope. You don't need to amass wealth and put your trust in uncertain riches. You don't need to embrace short-term values and goals, play safe and avoid danger. You can spread the message of God's lavish grace to a blind and suffering world, knowing that he who has world history in his hands is with you. He will receive us to glory with great rejoicing, a faultless, spotless bride. The banquet is prepared. The bridegroom is coming soon. We who had nothing to commend us and everything to disqualify us are invited to enter in and participate in the consummation of the ages.

Grace sets you free from the fear of condemnation. It prevents the church from being introverted and preoccupied with rulebook religion. Grace assures you that God has fully accepted you, has always loved you and always will. You are safe and you are free.

God calls you to arise and shine and put on your beautiful garments. Not only that, he calls you to go with good news for the nations, catching the evangelistic passion of Charles Wesley's famous hymn:

> Oh, that the world might taste and see
> The riches of His grace!
> The arms of love that compass me
> Would all mankind embrace.

Grace should never lead to passivity, but to outrageous adventure, a lifestyle that baffles those who play safe. It threatens the status quo not only of tentative religion, but also of cynical unbelief. It sets the church free to risk all for the praise of him who freely gave all for us.

A favourite missionary story of mine is the short biography of the young American martyrs, John and Betty Stam, who were dispatched to glory by the sword of a Chinese Communist soldier in December 1934, while their tiny baby girl was miraculously preserved (see Mrs Howard Taylor, *The Triumph of John and Betty Stam*, Philadelphia: China Inland Mission, 1960). A poem, written by another China Inland Mission missionary, was sent by John Stam to his parents. It was delivered to them on the day they received news of John and Betty's death. It illustrates our glorious freedom in the light of the assurance of future grace.

John wrote that he knew very well the danger that confronted them, but added that he was not afraid and that the enclosed poem fully expressed his feelings.

Afraid? Of what?
To feel the spirit's glad release?
To pass from pain to perfect peace?
The strife and strain of life to cease?
Afraid? – of that?

Afraid? Of what?
A flash – a crash – a pierced heart;
Darkness – light – O heaven's art!
A wound of His a counterpart!
Afraid? – of that?

Afraid? Of what?
To do by death what life could not –
Baptise with blood a stony plot,
Until souls shall blossom from the spot?
Afraid? – of that?

Afraid? Of what?
Afraid to see the Saviour's face
To hear His welcome and to trace
The glory gleam from wounds of grace?
Afraid? – of that?

(unpublished)

Assured of our acceptance with God through his wonderful grace, we can go unafraid to the waiting nations. "And this gospel of the kingdom shall be preached in the whole world for a witness to all the nations, and then the end shall come" (Matthew 24:14). The worldwide work of grace will be accomplished. Around the throne of God every nation, tribe and tongue will be represented. Eternal ages will unfold in the presence of our ever-gracious king.

"Now to him who is able to keep you from stumbling, and to make you stand in the presence of his glory blameless with great joy, to the only God our Saviour, through Jesus Christ our Lord, be glory, majesty, dominion and authority, before all time and now and for ever. Amen" (Jude verses 24–25).

Bibliography

Bridges, Jerry, *The Discipline of Grace*, NavPress, 1994

Carson, D A, *A Call to Spiritual Reformation*, Baker, 1992

Carson, D A, *The Cross and Christian Ministry*, Baker, 1993

Carson, D A, *The Gospel According to John,* Eerdmans, 1991

Cormack, Don, *Killing Fields, Living Fields,* Monarch Books/OMF International, 1997

Fee, Gordon D, *God's Empowering Presence,* Hendrickson, 1994

Fee, Gordon D, *Paul's Letter to the Philippians*, NICNT, Eerdmans, 1995

Hays, Richard B, *The Moral Vision of the New Testament*, T & T Clark, 1997

Hodge, Charles, *The First Epistle to the Corinthians*, Banner of Truth, 1959

Kidner, Derek, *Proverbs,* IVP, 1972

Lloyd-Jones, D Martyn, *Romans: The New Man, An Exposition of Chapter 6,* Banner of Truth Trust, 1972

Lloyd-Jones, D Martyn, *Spiritual Depression: Its Causes and Cure,* Pickering and Inglis, 1965

Lloyd-Jones, D Martyn, *The Final Perseverance of the Saints, Romans 8:17–39*, Banner of Truth Trust, 1975

Lloyd-Jones, D Martyn, *The Law, Romans 7:1 – 8:4,* Banner of Truth Trust, 1973

Milne, Bruce, *The Message of Heaven and Hell*, IVP, 2002

Moo, Douglas, *The Epistle to the Romans*, NICNT, Eerdmans, 1996

Motyer, Alec, *The Prophecy of Isaiah,* IVP, 1993

Peterson, Eugene H, *The Message: The Bible in Contemporary Language,* NavPress, 2002

Phillips, J B, *Letters to Young Churches*, Fontana, 1947

Piper, John, *Future Grace,* Multnomah, 1995

Schreiner, Thomas R, *Paul, Apostle of God's Glory in Christ* IVP, 2001

Stott, John, *Calling Christian Leaders,* IVP, 2002

Taylor, Mrs Howard, *The Triumph of John and Betty Stam,* Philadelphia: CIM, 1960

Wright, N T, *The Climax of the Covenant,* T & T Clark, 1991

Newfrontiers

Newfrontiers is a worldwide family of churches on a mission to establish the kingdom of God by:

- restoring the church
- making disciples
- training leaders
- planting churches

For more information please visit our website at: www.new-frontiers.xtn.org or contact:

Newfrontiers
17 Clarendon Villas
Hove
East Sussex BN3 3RE
United Kingdom
Phone: (+44) 1273–234555
Fax: (+44) 1273–234556
Email: office@newfrontiers.xtn.org